"Coach Tim Fanning's latest book, *Serve to Lead 2*, continues to shine light on who and what is important in life. And believe me, it's not always what this world wants you to believe. His faith, coupled with his numerous mission trips and then his intense battle with cancer, has given him a unique perspective that we can all learn from and aspire to reach. This book inspires the heck out of me and I'm so blessed to call Coach Fanning my friend."

-**Tim Hudson**
17 Year MLB Veteran, 4-Time All-Star,
Atlanta Braves Hall of Fame

"Tim Fanning, one of the great young high school baseball coaches in America today, has hit a "Homerun" with his book, Serve To Lead 2. Outlining his "Life Lessons" intertwined with his own serious life threatening health issues, he has created an honest look at what really matters in the life of a coach. His faith in GOD, love of family, love of extended family of players and his community shines throughout. The old adage of "one good service to others returns 10 fold" is vivid! He has served many! May GOD continue to Bless him and his extended families! Thanks, Coach Tim!"

-**Gene Stephenson**
3rd Winningest Coach in NCAA DI History,
College World Series - 7 Times, Wichita State University

"Tim – thank you for sharing God's path for your life with the world. What a great motivation for those who want to make a difference and are looking for a purpose. Tim's journey reminds us of the influential people in our lives and how impactful small acts of kindness can have on people we interact with daily. I personally picked up lessons throughout to share and enjoyed hearing how God has worked through Tim as a coach, father, husband and missionary. *Serve to Lead 2* has refocused my intention to be a better servant and more yielding to God's perfect plan."

-**Butch Thompson**
Auburn University Head Baseball Coach,
2019 College World Series

I would like to dedicate this book to my wife, Renee and my daughters, Brianna and Macie. They have been my saving grace. They love me unconditionally and no matter what the circumstances, their presence makes me a better man!

SERVE TO
LEAD$_2$

Copyright © 2021 by Tim Fanning

All rights reserved. No portion of this book may be reproduced, stored in a retrieval system, or transmitted in any form or by any means - electronic, mechanical, photography, recording, scanning, or other - except for brief quotations in critical reviews or articles, without the prior written permission of the publisher.

TO LEARN MORE, VISIT:
SERVETOLEAD2.COM

SERVE TO
LEAD₂

TIM FANNING

CONTENTS

Introduction 9
1. The Dreaded "C" Word 13
2. Angels on Earth 49
3. Life of Service 57
4. God's Path 63
5. Panama 77
6. Africa 97
7. Colombia 105
8. Dominican Republic 113
9. Costa Rica 125
10. Taiwan 131
11. Puerto Rico 139
12. Self-Pity 149
13. Coaching Coaches 159
14. Magical Seasons 169
15. Off the Field 191
16. The Year 207
17. Humbled Beginnings 217
18. Dirt Road 227
About The Author 233

INTRODUCTION

I think more often than not when we search for answers to life's little mysteries, we are looking in the wrong places. We seek insite from famous people, television shows or radio personalities. Don't get me wrong, there are inspirational bursts from all of these places. People rise from poverty, personal tragedy or disabilities to achieve great success and all of a sudden their stardom makes us pay attention. Were they not the same people before they were famous? My point is that we are surrounded by these people every day and for some reason we don't see them.

The fact of the matter is just about everything that I have built my life on was so graciously given to me by people you've never heard of and I would venture to say you never will. We are so consumed with what we are fed on social and main stream media we fail to realize we are walking in fields of gold every day surrounded by nuggets of life that can sustain you for all your days. All you have to do is pay attention and the blueprint is there to follow. What am I taking about? I am talking about "servants"! They will teach you all you need to know and there will be plenty left-over to teach others.

Sometimes these people are hard to see because they don't want to be seen. They operate behind the scenes with no fan-fare or any desire to be recognized. A single mother that works three jobs and never buys anything for herself. A little league coach that buys cleats and a glove for one of his players without anyone knowing.

A co-worker that stops to ask you about your family when he/she is up against a project deadline at work. A bus driver that greets every kid with a smile regardless of what's going on in his/her life. A coach that stays after practice to talk to one of his/her players about life despite his wife/husband and children waiting at home. The socially awkward kid that finds the courage to tell the starting quarterback he really enjoyed watching him play on Friday night. Of course, the soldier that straps his boots on every day with no hesitation and provides the very freedom for us that we many times take for granted.

The list of examples could go on forever but I think you get the point. All these people serve others and in return they expect nothing! People seem to be starving for inspiration and all they have to do is look around. No it's not sexy but it's the very foundation for life that has meaning. Serving others plants seeds in countless lives and when watered often produce leaders without us even knowing.

Over the course of this book I will share what I have experienced while serving others, give examples of remarkable selflessness from people all over the world and attempt to give thanks to so many that have poured themselves into me without ever asking for anything in return. My goal is to hopefully inspire people to embrace putting others ahead of themselves and know that by doing this, their lives will have a much greater purpose and in turn empower others to achieve more than they ever imagined possible!

SERVE!

CHAPTER 1
THE DREADED "C" WORD

Chances are if you are reading this book, you have been affected by cancer in some way, shape or form. An uncle, aunt, grandparents, nieces, nephews, friends or even fought the battle yourself. It is such a relentless disease that shows no mercy. Race or religion is not a factor, size or shape doesn't matter and age is certainly not a parameter. You can look and feel as healthy as ever and it will not shield you from this "Beast!" It hunts 24 hours a day, 7 days a week and has unlimited fuel to wreak havoc on this world with impunity.

I first learned I had Colon Cancer on July 30th, 2019. A few weeks earlier, I had just returned from an amazing mission trip to the Dominican Republic. I remember feeling such peace and a sense of accomplishment after this trip. Not that the other 20 mission trips I had been on before had less meaning but I just felt God was truly leading me in a direction I had never felt before. One of my dearest friends, Payton, that went on that trip, even told me he had never seen me that happy during a trip before and if anyone would know that, it would be him. He has been on eight trips with me and has always been a rock for me.

The summer was coming to an end, school was about to crank up and as always I was excited about what new lives I could impact through service. Of course, there were administrative duties that included scheduling, eligibility and facility improvements but the prospect of my 21st year coaching was just as exciting, if not more than my first year. That's what I have always loved about serving others. It never gets old because you have a chance to change lives every day.

Little did I know my life was about to change forever. I guess in all honesty, maybe I knew something was wrong. I noticed some differences in my bowel movements but nothing a stubborn man that never goes to the doctor would call serious. I never went to the doctor growing up. Besides the fact we didn't have insurance, I just thought people went for stitches and broken bones. Even then, who couldn't get by with a few broken fingers or toes, just tape them up! I don't take medicine and to be honest we pretty much have raised our kids that way.

I did however, notice that breaks while cutting the grass seemed to come with more frequency. Now living in the deep south in July gives you a built in excuse because the heat index is regularly around 100 degrees, but my wife even noticed. There are a lot of things my wife has done for me over the years to make my life better (probably too many to count) but making me go to the doctor I guess ranks #1. Everything since that day has kind of been a blur.

I remember thinking when I returned from the D.R. that summer, my vision for life outside of teaching and coaching was crystal clear. I was so certain of the platform God had blessed me with to reach others. Well, as is the case more times than not, God's plan is not necessarily our plan. So over the next several weeks, my days consisted of doctor's appointments and my nights consisted of sleeplessness. It's very difficult to explain how much your mind wanders and never shuts off, it is in a constant state of motion.

Will I be able to coach again? How am I going to travel the world and share a message of hope? Who is going to take care of my girls if something happens? I may never see my daughters walk down the aisle and daddy have that first dance! Can I make it to my 25th wedding anniversary? What about my girl's college education? Am I going to wilt away to nothing physically? I still have so much to do!

I have always somewhat struggled with the idea that there will never be enough time to accomplish all I have set out to do in this lifetime. As William Wallace said, "Every man dies, not every man really lives." Those words have resonated with me my entire adult life. They have always pushed me to take chances, be bold, not care what people think and live life as hard and as fast as possible. So for someone with that mindset, I struggled greatly at first with how much my life began to slow down. I would say it took me a few months to truly come to terms with surrendering to God's will and realize the only thing I could control was my attitude. I would like to share this year and a half long journey with you in hopes that you can see this dreaded disease through my eyes but at the same time try my best to show you how God's grace and the beautiful spirit of others can deliver anyone from the darkest places imaginable.

During the first month, there were MRI's, CT's and Pet scans. In an addition to the massive tumor in my colon, they determined I had cancer in my lymph nodes as well, prompting the doctor's to categorize me as Stage 4. Before I could start chemo treatments, I had surgeries to remove a lymph node from my groin, implant a power port for treatments and give me an ileostomy. This was done because my surgeon felt that the tumor in my colon was so large, she feared it could rupture during the course of treatments and then we would have a huge problem.

I am sure many of you are not familiar with this procedure, I sure wasn't at the time. They basically cut your stomach open, take out part of your intestine and place it on the outside of your stomach. There is a bag you put over it to catch all the bile before it gets to your colon. I know that doesn't paint a pretty picture but I feel it's necessary for you to understand that it's not just the fact you have cancer, it's everything that comes along with it while you are fighting the disease. This was probably the biggest hurdle I faced mentally during this battle.

This procedure along with the extraction of the lymph node prevented me from working out, swimming and laying out in the sun. That may not seem like much but for me it made me feel like a prisoner and looking back on it now, there were a lot of self-inflicted wounds. I didn't lay out in the sun because I didn't want people to see my ostomy bag and I didn't because it made me feel uncomfortable not because I wasn't physically able. I had to spend six days in the hospital, miss the first football game of the year and anyone that knows me, I don't miss! I was battling a pity party every time I turned around.

But, I also remember that last night in the hospital like it was yesterday. I finally started to realize that I was not in this alone and even more importantly excepting the fact that I could not do this alone. I am admittedly a stubborn person by nature and patience has never been one of my virtues. Even though all week my friends drove three hours to see me in that hospital, it wasn't until late that Friday night I started to truly see what was happening around me. See God had put me specifically where I needed to be for the last 20 years so this amazing school and community could wrap their arms around me and my family.

Coach Gibson (our football coach) and several players called me after the game and told me they had dedicated the game and victory to me. Not to mention, we had not beaten that school in football since the late 70's. I just sat in that extremely uncomfortable hospital bed and cried like a baby. Those tears began to wash my self-pity away and transform my thought process. Of course, that next Thursday at the pep rally, the team presented me with the signed game ball. I had no words, only tears. I side note from that day; my wife sent me a picture of that day almost a year later to the exact day and I looked like a POW that had been in prisoned for years. She made sure to bring that up when I was complaining about being overweight.

After healing from surgery, I finally started chemo. I would go on a Tuesday and receive about a six-hour transfusion and then leave with a pump hooked to me for the next two days. On Thursday around lunch time, they would unhook me and I would head home. Every one of us have friends and I am sure like everyone else, you have what you would consider your inner circle. These are people you know without a shadow of doubt, you can depend on day or night, no matter what the circumstance. What I didn't realize was how many people truly cared about me and my family.

It's not easy to ask someone to completely drop what they are doing, drive you an hour and half, sit with you for at least six hours, sometimes longer and then drive you back an hour and half. That's what was so humbling, I didn't have to ask. They would sit there and watch me sleep, watch me get sick, go get me food if I could eat and for me became my guardian angels. Not only that, Curtis Howard, one of our volunteers, has an extensive medical background and he would always keep me off the ledge. His late night phone calls were always so positive and his expertise provided such comfort to me. He always found a way to perfectly balance truth and encouragement. I've since tried to tell them how much I truly appreciate their sacrifice but I don't think words can ever fully quantify my love for these amazing people.

It wasn't just chemo treatments; it was three hour drives to UAB for tests. The thing about getting tests, is the stress that comes with awaiting the results. You don't know if the treatments have been working, you only know how they have made you feel physically which is like a walking zombie with no energy. My wife would always go with me for test results and every time, Kelly Allison was there, making us laugh and keeping us positive. That is truly a gift God has given her, I am sure, without her even knowing. She always brightens the room and as far as everyone knows at UAB and the Montgomery Cancer Center, she is my sister!

Now, one thing I never did during this process was get on the internet and look for information. I didn't want to hear about survival percentages, chemo horror stories and chances for physical recovery. My whole life, I have always considered myself an outlier. No one was ever going to tell me I couldn't do something so for me mentally, that's how I had to approach this battle. I waited for my hair to fall out and waited to shrink up because that's what I was told could happen in my chemo education classes but it never happened. I was extremely tired, had some skin irritations and a few allergic reactions during my transfusions but nothing I couldn't handle. It did make me feel good when my doctor's continued to be surprised by my weight gain and my cancer marker continuing to decrease in number.

In the big scheme of things, I didn't really know what any of that meant but I didn't care. I was focused on one week at a time. You see, I get myself in trouble mentally when I look too far ahead. It's natural for me, I have always been a planner and a dreamer but I realized early on in this process, that only brought me to dark places. I would try to map everything out on a calendar so I could start planning mission trips, coaching clinics, off-season/pre-season workout schedules and day-by-day I finally realized I was not in control. That word "Control" comes up a lot during a battle of this magnitude. It makes you second guess everything and if you don't surrender to God's will, the devil will take your mind to places you don't ever want to go.

When I had those struggles, one place I could always seek for comfort was school. Just walking on campus, seeing those kids, the faculty and my players always put me back where I needed to be. Something I also think gets lost is how important your chemo team is during this process. Mine in particular, I call them the "Four Horseman"; Paige, April, Haley and Ashley. I cannot begin to tell you how positive these ladies were for me every time I was there and I know how hard it is for them. They are surrounded everyday by patients in dire circumstances that they may never get to say goodbyes to. They go out of there way not only to provide the best medical care possible but to know you as a person. They get to know your family and if you don't have someone to talk to, you can always count on them to lend you an ear.

See I consider them the end of the line. Like I said early, I was definitely not familiar with the medical system but after going through this process, I have seen how compartmentalized and cold it can be sometimes. A lot of times you feel like cattle being herded through the slaughter house. Maybe is has to be that way but it feels very impersonal at times. The orders come from the surgical team, you are poked and prodded until you just want to say the heck with this crap. That's why what these nurses do is so vital to your success. They see what it does to you physically. They have to stop your treatments when it gets too bad, they have help you to the bathroom because can barely walk and most importantly they sympathize with you. I like to compare it to big company CEO's that institute rules but very rarely see how it affects the boots on the ground. Have you ever watched the show Undercover Boss? If so, you know exactly what I am talking about.

Don't get me wrong, my surgeon at UAB, Karin Hardiman is one of the best in the world and when we are one-on-one, I feel a true connection but there are a lot of layers between her and the "boots on the ground". I felt the same way about my lead nurse at UAB, Jennifer Brown. If I ever needed anything, she was there for me and she could make things happen. If there were scheduling conflicts, if they were backlogged in imaging or getting prescriptions, she always had my back. I don't know if she had to beg, borrow and steal but she always came through for me like a "boss"! I bet it was like herding cats sometimes for her but you would have never known it because she was always so positive and really had a calming effect on me during some pretty stressful times.

I have been told by people that there has to be a disconnect for surgeons dealing with life and death situations so they don't get too close. I just don't know that world, I try to do everything in my power to get as close as I can to the people that surround me. If any of my doctor's seem distant when talking to me, the only thing I know to do is go right at them. They may leave my room calling me names but they will never doubt my resolve or the fact that I tried my hardest to know them on a personal level.

I have always been that way though. It doesn't matter if I am around so called "famous people", business tycoons, legends in the coaching industry or professional athletes you are always going to get the same guy. I have always felt if the air is cold in the room, make them feel uncomfortable and they only have two choices. They have to dismiss themselves or engage you. More often than not, they will engage because they respect your effort and status becomes non-existent. Because, let's be honest, everyone no matter their title, social status, or wealth are all looking for the same thing when they wake-up each and every morning: purpose! It shapes our attitudes, facial expressions, body language, energy and most of all, how we treat others.

During my first four months of chemo, there were a lot of up and downs but like I mentioned earlier, I could always count on the Glenwood family and this entire community to raise my spirits to heights I never expected during this ordeal. It was very overwhelming at first because the amount of phone calls, text messages and emails that were coming in every day. This included people from all over the world; from Taiwan, Africa, the Caribbean, South and Central America. Former teammates in high school and college began to reach out, college coaches from all over the country, not to mention players and former parents that numbered in the thousands. I had to have a team to answer questions and keep people updated as much as possible. These people will never fully know the impact they had on me then and are still having on me today. There is not a day that goes by that I still don't get text messages and phone calls from people checking on me.

During the football season, the Booster Club, the Foundation and the school sold wrist bands and shirts in my honor for Colon Cancer night vs Autauga Academy. I was told we were going to meet at the 50-yard line to pray before the game for me and Scott Tubbs from Autauga that was also battling colon cancer. So I walked out with my family and Scott was with his family, coaches and their football team but I noticed our football team had not made it back to the field after warm-ups yet. It was a little strange but events don't always happen exactly how you plan them so I didn't think too much about it and then the football team busted out of the fieldhouse with brand new blue uniforms (which are not our colors). They all surrounded me and my family and then the Pastor made an unexpected announcement. "Any one that would like to come down and pray with us for these two men, come on down." Not that I wasn't already a puddle of tears, when I finally had the courage to look up, I don't know if anyone was left in the stands because all I saw was a wad of humanity making their way to the field. I was later given a framed picture from that night and it looked like half of the field was covered with people, amazing! Oh and by the way, the team presented me and Coach Tubbs with our own personalized jerseys and the neck was inscribed, "Serve something greater than yourselves".

Later, I also found out that they sold almost a thousand shirts and I can't tell you how many wrist bands. I still get a great big smile on my face when I see people wearing them after all these months have gone by. If the night wasn't special enough, after the game finally got started, I was walking back towards the press box and someone stopped me. It was my Little League coach. He preceded to tell me that this was the first Friday night he has missed as a football official in almost thirty years but there was no way he was going to miss this event. So I kissed him on the top of his bald head and cried for about an hour.

In January 2020, I was able to attend the Alabama Baseball Coaches Association State Convention. Normally that would not be a topic for a lot of discussion because I have been doing that for about 20 years, but this one was definitely different. First of all, I was so excited to just leave the house and be with my coaching staff in an environment that made me feel normal again. Second of all, I got to see so many of the coaches around the state that had been calling, texting and praying for me. Barry Dean, the Executive Director, scheduled me to speak for a few minutes following a local doctor, his topic; Colon Cancer! His speech was very informative and what a tremendous topic for Barry to approve in light of what Coach Tubbs and I were battling at the time. It really meant a lot to me that he would do that. If you have ever been to conventions before, you know that as one speaker finishes, the other makes his/her way to the stage to speak and while this transpires, the audience chooses to stay for the next speaker or seek entertainment elsewhere. Well to my surprise, there were few people leaving and a lot of people coming in. Now, everyone that speaks to big groups would like to tell you that their material is amazing and it would be impossible for someone not to get something out of what they are speaking on but let's be honest, that's just not the case. It doesn't matter if the material is earth shattering and the delivery is flawless, you are not going to reach everyone nor will you hold everyone's attention.

When you have a room full of people that number in the hundreds or in the thousands, the fact still remains, everyone in that room is different from the person sitting next to them. Their minds are all in different places at that exact moment, which includes: professionally, physically, personally and even spiritually. Their minds could be anywhere but there at that particular point in time. If you ask me, my goal has always been to genuinely impact one person in that room. See there is a difference between "listening" and "hearing". If you can get one person to actually hear what you are saying, you can change a life and in this world that seems at most times surrounded by nothing but "noise"; you may have made a change in someone's life that cannot be quantified. Unlike any other topic I have ever spoke on, without a doubt all I focused on was reaching at least one person because I wanted to save a life! If I could get just one person to get tested earlier than they would have before they entered that banquet room, mission accomplished. Now when you have a room full of guys that coach for a living and pretty much as stubborn a group of people on the planet (me included), it's not necessarily as easy as one might think. Nevertheless, my goal was clear and the only thing I could do was pour my heart out. So that's what I did.

I told them, I never thought in a million years, I would be standing in front of them for this reason. Not me, I hike volcanoes, I travel the world, I swim with whale sharks, I win championships, I have a beautiful family, I have the best job in the world! See that's the thing, it's not going to happen to you, until it does. I have never been more engaged with a group of people in my entire life. It's very rare to literally watch people's facial expressions change within an instant. It felt like every person I made eye contact with had a huge spotlight on them and they were the only person in that room. I shared how disappointed I was in myself after I realized how I had been fast forwarding through life. The next project, the next assignment, the next trip, the next meeting, always; "the next thing!" The biggest thing I learned in that first six months, be intentional with your time. Be *intentional* with your wife, your kids, your co-workers, your students, your parents, your siblings and especially your relationship with Jesus!

Everyone reading this has been told or read somewhere in a book at some point in your life:

You are never guaranteed tomorrow!

Live tomorrow like it's your last!

Live every day to the fullest!

Seize the day!

Carpe diem!

I am quite sure there are hundreds of these phrases that trigger impulses in our souls that make us want to be better people. They make us draft our "bucket list". They change the way we look at the world for brief moments in time. They make us want to live a healthier lifestyle, read more books, attend church more and volunteer more in your community. I have always prided myself on being that guy but it's much deeper than that. I have more bucket lists than you can shake a stick at and a quite impressive library full of books that have inspired me over the years. If we are not "intentional" with our time, all of it will eventually fade like theatre lights as the final curtain comes down. Can you imagine if all of us committed to being intentional with our time; what types of truly magnificent relationships would develop. Because at the end of day when that final horn sounds, that's all that really matters. I know it sounds impossible and daunting but what if? What if?

After speaking to the coaches, Mark Jackson, a local Pastor and former high school coach came on stage and asked if he could pray for me. He asked me to step down off the stage so people could lay hands on me during the prayer and as before just like during the Autauga football game, people just kept coming. Again, sobbing like a baby, I felt so unbelievably special that God had placed these amazing men and that moment in my life. I can promise you this, the best moments in your life will always be ones that are unexpected, unplanned and completely out of your control. That's why they are so pure and have the greatest impact on you. You don't have time to mess it up with your own thoughts of what it should look like or feel like. How many times do we sabotage ourselves in that way? I just sat there in front of that stage an allowed God's grace to pour over me like a warm blanket. I felt so loved, so protected and so proud to be in a room full of men that put my needs ahead of their own!

After that amazing weekend, pre-season was in full swing. As in the past, when returning from clinics, we know the start of the season is just around the corner. The coaches are all fired up, the parents are in a fever pitch and the players have such anticipation for the games to start. For me personally, it was definitely different than any other season because of my limitations physically. Not just being so worn out from chemo treatments but not being able to throw at full speed or swing a bat with intensity made me feel very inadequate at times. I will tell you this, no matter how I felt physically, every day I left that practice field, my heart was full of joy and it didn't hurt that my boy Don Griffin had installed me a personal heater in the dugout! Once the season started that became very popular and I mean very popular. I would look in from the 3rd base coaching box and there would be a line of players trying to get some of that precious heat.

As I was building our program, I knew the alumni would play a crucial role in our success but what I didn't realize was just how important they would be to me personally. That love and passion for this school transitioned to me when I was diagnosed with cancer. I spoke earlier on how so many of them reached out to me on a daily basis during my darkest times but what I didn't tell you about was the reunion we had right before that season started. Several parents from previous and current players organized the entire event. There were close to 300 people that came out to support their coach. They were selling raffle tickets for amazing prizes so graciously donated by people and companies from all over our community. Their sole purpose was to raise money for me and my family. We had great barbecue and even better fellowship. It was a little overwhelming to see that many familiar faces all at once. There were so many stories told; some embellished more than others but never the less, it was such a proud moment for me personally. All the different classes got together to take pictures afterwards and of course all the facilities were open for anyone and everyone that wanted a tour. To be perfectly honest we could have stayed there all night and it would have been fine by me.

I was supposed to speak for about twenty minutes and I spoke for about forty-five. It probably could have been twice that. I was just so fired up and extremely honored to be up there in front of this amazing group of people. Prior to that season starting, I remember so many people asking me if I was going to coach that season. Are you going to be able to handle it while on chemo? Will you be able to hold up physically from the surgeries? To be honest, that thought never crossed my mind for a single moment! How in the world could I let those kids down like that? This night just confirmed what I already knew; I was exactly where I was supposed to be!

Now as all of you know, the Spring of 2020 will forever be remembered in history. That's a pretty big statement and usually that word "forever" is used way too often and is certainly not used correctly but this time, it is true. Our history books will one day tell the story, documentaries will certainly be made and generations will pass down historic tales of tragedy and triumph from the great COVID pandemic. Now as I shared with you earlier, I am not big on getting information from the internet and certainly not from mainstream media these days because it's as confusing as a calculus equation, not to mention wading through everyone's bias opinion. So as a leader of young men and women they are constantly looking to you for direction. What does this mean? What does that mean? Are we going to be able to play? Is school going to be cancelled?

Will we get to graduate? What about prom? What about Senior Day?

As an adult, many of these questions can seem trivial at the time because we have already experienced some form of all these things but as a sixteen, seventeen or eighteen year-old, it's a pretty darn big deal! The only thing I could tell them was, "I don't know, but I do know, whatever we do will be together. We are going to show up every day, work as hard as we can, love one another and submit to God's will." I am blessed to be around extremely smart, passionate, hard-working kids that to be honest, probably know me better than I know myself. Most times they know what I am going to say before I even say it but this Spring I was desperately trying to hide my own anxiety from them. I was trying so hard not to be selfish in my own wants and desires because of how great they made me feel during a very dark time.

I didn't care if it was freezing and people who know me, know I can't stand cold weather. I didn't care if it was raining, which I believed it rained more that Winter than any year of my coaching career, it only mattered that we were together. So I was as honest as possible updating them on what I knew and we just played ball until they said we couldn't play ball anymore. We had two overnight trips which I think helped get their minds off things. Nothing like hanging with your boys on the road to make you feel normal again. One of those trips turned out to be the last time we would play and also one of the most memorable days of my life.

We were at the Autauga Wood Bat Tournament playing against my friend and Colon Cancer warrior, Scott Tubbs. The Montgomery Advertiser was there to do a story on Scott and I. That didn't really seem unusual to me because I had done several media outlet requests prior to the season starting. Renee and Macie had made their way over from her tournament across town which seemed a little odd but who cared, they were at my game. When you coach baseball and your daughter plays softball, you have to get very creative sometimes just to get a brief glimpse of her playing or vice versa. Well the game was about to start, time for line-up exchange, anthem and prayer.

I have never been a coach that makes the line-up prior to getting to the field, to each his own. I always want a feel for the team that day, a gut feeling about a guy maybe, injuries may arise or even knucklehead shenanigans could occur. Man I love my job! I tell you this because with the unexpected interview before the game thrown into the mix, the umpires and Coach Tubbs were waiting for me at the plate. In my haste trying to get out there, I never even noticed that Autauga was in blue jerseys (not their colors) for Colon Cancer Awareness. Just like back in the Fall during football season, these jerseys weren't some throw together last minute item, obviously a lot of thought had been put in to it. They were sweet!

Now what I haven't told you is that back in the fall, Coach Tubbs called me and said he wanted to show me something. So he sent me a picture of their hats that his seniors designed. The hat had his number #8 and my number #6 on the back with the Colon

Cancer symbol. I said, "man that's awesome" and started laughing out loud. He said, "why are you laughing?" So I sent him a picture and it was the same thing. We had put that on the back of our hats as well. It was a great moment, not only because we had the same thoughts, but I think we realized despite our mental and physical struggles (mostly mental), that we would always be there for each other and more importantly; our players had our back too!

So I made my way towards the plate, we exchanged line-ups and wouldn't know it, there were several people making their way on to the field. They got me again! Our State Association's Athletic Director, the Executive Director of Alabama Baseball Coaches Association, the rep from BSN Sports that had the jerseys done and representatives from Waterbreak Ministries. Coach Tubbs presented me with a personalized jersey and it even had my non-profit logo on the sleeve. That blew me away. We prayed in front of that crowd and every one of his players came up to hug me. Now that I realized the jokes on me, my wife and daughter were smiling from ear to ear. I guess in my old age the wool is becoming easier to pull over my eyes. See, I am the one over the years that always came up with surprise trips, tickets to athletic events, birthday parties, gifts, etc. It just made me feel so alive to do these things for other people but now that the shoe has been on the other foot, I am not going to lie, it feels pretty amazing too.

That's the thing about love, it has no limitations what so ever when it is unconditional. During this journey it has been shown to me around every corner I turn. Just when I start to feel "normal" again in my mind, God says, "Wait a minute buddy, I am not done with you yet"! That's what a lot of people don't understand, God's grace is so much bigger than we can ever possible comprehend. He has so much more for our lives than we can imagine in our wildest dreams but most of us are too stubborn or scared to just submit to his will. We put limitations on ourselves from the time we are born but God has no limitations. People don't do this on purpose, it's in our nature and embedded in us by the devil to avoid embarrassment. It's called *pride* and it has no place at the right hand of the father!

By the way, in case you were wondering, we were down by one in the last inning, scratched two and snatched victory from jaws of defeat. That was as excited as I have been for a regular season victory in a really long time, maybe ever. That weekend went by so fast, probably because it was our last of the season. Let the quarantine begin. Now as sad as I was to have this unprecedented stoppage, what it did do was allow me to concentrate on the biggest surgery of my life. About the same time that we were getting shut down, while receiving radiation treatments, I developed an infection from a perforation in my tumor. My surgeon decided it was time to go in and get it out. This way she would be able to get any of the infection as well.

I think it's important to be as descriptive as possible so you may understand where my mind was at during this process. The goals for the surgery were:

1. Remove the tumor from my colon.

2. Remove any infected lymph nodes that were accessible.

3 Remove any infection that still existed from the perforation.

4. Reverse the ileostomy I currently had in place.

5. Re-attach the colon so it would be functional.

6. Add a colostomy bag so the colon could have time to heal.

As you know, there is no way of knowing how it went until you wake-up. That uncertainty can lead to a lot of anxiety prior to surgery, especially one of this magnitude with so many variables. Now, couple that with the fact that my wife was not allowed to stay with me due to COVID restrictions, so to be honest, I was just plain scared. The calm before the storm happens in pre-op as you are being prepped by the nurses, techs and the anesthesiologist. It's freezing cold, your mind is racing so fast you feel like you are at a NASCAR race. The only thing I knew to do was pray and request to speak to my surgeon before I was taken to the operating room.

I have never been afraid to speak my mind and I wasn't going to start now. I wanted her to know how much faith I had in her. I told her that I would earn every minute of life she could give me and I promised she would be proud of the man I would strive to be. It was very emotional and not just for me. What I said earlier about people's opinions that surgeons have to keep their distance from patients to be the best they can be, well not on that day and not with my surgeon. I will never forget that and she will never know how much trust that brief moment created. Boy did I need it.

I woke up in my hospital room alone with a catheter attached to me, a drain tube coming out of my stomach and it felt like someone had hit me in my stomach with a baseball bat. It was definitely the loneliest I had ever felt in my life. When I finally had the strength to hold my head up and look down at my mid-section, my heart just sunk. It wasn't the staples that ran from the very bottom of my abdomen all the way up to my belly button, it was the extra bag I now had attached to the other side of my stomach. I definitely didn't realize they were going to filet me open that much but all I could think about was that bag. I just laid there staring at the wall, not knowing if something went wrong and exactly what that meant because I hadn't spoken to anyone. This went on for hours but it felt like days. I tried to go back to sleep just to avoid thinking about it but as you know when something that heavy is weighing on your mind, sleep is usually not an option.

Dr. Hardiman finally came by to see me which in retrospect probably wasn't that long. She explained to me how hard the surgery was and that it took almost seven hours. She had gotten the tumor, all the infection, inserted a stint in my bladder but was not able to reconnect the colon as we discussed and felt it was necessary to give me the colostomy. With the amount of blood, they had to give me during surgery and the elapsed time, she just didn't feel comfortable proceeding any further. I could tell by the look on her face that it was definitely tougher than she anticipated but just like life, you never really know how hard it's going to be until you take the field. You can read about it all you want, people can tell you all about it but it's not real until you step in that batter's box and that 90 mph fastball is coming at you!

I could tell she was exhausted and left everything she had on that operating table. I could also see the disappointment on her face that it didn't go as planned because she knew how much it meant to me and what my expectations were. But here's the thing, all of our lives are filled with expectations, if they weren't, we would all end up nowhere. We have to have them but we also have to deal with life when things fall short of our expectations. Yes, I was disappointed, yes I was a little pissed off and yes I was alone but what was I going to do, quit? I have been pushing my players for over twenty years and the overwhelming message during all that time has been to never give up and never let anyone tell you that you can't do something.

So that's what I did. I got out of that bed as soon as I could and started walking. If there wasn't somebody there to walk with me, I walked by myself and wrote it on the board. I went to the bathroom and cleaned up with all those things attached to me. I ordered food three times a day. I didn't care about any of that stuff, all I knew is I needed to get home and be with my family. The only way you do that in my situation is to show the doctor's you can eat, walk and that your vitals are good. So for four days that's what I did. I really didn't want to talk to anyone. I didn't want anyone telling me it was going to be ok. I just wanted to turn the page and for me that was getting out of that hospital. I went home two days' sooner than when I had the ileostomy surgery and it wasn't even in the same stratosphere as this surgery.

I am not going to sit here and tell you it was all roses when I got home because it wasn't. It was a tough recovery process both physically and mentally but having my beautiful family around me every single day sure made it a whole lot easier. Whatever I needed, they provided, including a kick in the behind if I needed that too. I have raised some amazingly tough young ladies and my wife is the strongest woman I know, so feeling sorry for myself was not really an option. If I ever had those brief moments of self-pity or allowed my mind to wonder where it didn't belong, I made sure to do it when everyone was asleep. As I wrote about earlier, that's the real battle, the mind. You ask any doctor or someone that has battled this dreaded disease and they will tell you that having the right mindset, is the single biggest key to a successful recovery.

So over the next month, that's what I did. I would get up and walk for physical therapy. Most people don't realize exactly how much their core controls the entire body until it's taken away. There is no lifting, no yard work and everyday household chores that you take for granted are off the menu. Crazy how we end up really missing things, like taking out the trash! I knew it would get better day-by-day and it did. Two weeks later, I had to get my staples out and meet with Dr. Hardiman about the pathology report from the surgery. Again, I have no medical background and didn't stay at a Holiday Inn Express last night but I did know this report would be life-changing, one way or the other.

She sat down beside me and asked me how I was doing. I told her everything seemed to be working just fine with nominal pain and that I was not taking any pain medication. So she proceeded to pull out this piece of paper that looked like it had a million words on it. Of course, it didn't but to be honest everything at that point was a little fuzzy. She started talking and I didn't hear much except words that I couldn't pronounce so I just tried to take deep breaths until she finished. In the middle of that last breath, I heard the words, clear margins! I looked up and I saw an expression on Dr. Hardiman's face that quite frankly, I don't believe I had ever seen before. I could literally see the joy on her face as the words carefully came out of her mouth. Of course, then she left me so the screaming could begin as her Nurse Practitioner began to take all my staples out. I am definitely a sissy!

Josh McConnell was the chariot driver that day to and from Birmingham. Not really sure how I got him past the COVID police to share in that moment with me but I can lay it on pretty thick when I want something. Plus, I do recall being a pretty good actor in our high school Drama Department. All kidding aside, I was so thankful for his presence that day. That's a lot of windshield time when waiting for a destination that is unknown. He kept me relaxed and focused on what was going to be and not what could be. Now, after he saw the first couple staples cut out, he might have been regretting it. It was time to get home and share the news.

Well I figured since everyone seemed to be surprising me for about a year, it was my turn. I didn't call Renee to discuss the new findings but instead just sent her a text letting her know we were on the way back. Now, some of you may feel that is a little cruel but to be perfectly honest, I felt in my heart this type of news should only be delivered in person. She has been every bit apart of this as I have. She has felt every 10 blade, helped me change every ostomy bag, watched me not be able to hold my eyes open, lift my arms up or a few times even be able to talk. She changed her diet to fit mine, warmed my hands and feet when I had no feeling in them, encouraged me every time I was feeling like crap and listened patiently as I constantly complained about not being able to travel.

This piece of paper I had in my possession was every bit hers as it was mine. I remember walking in the house like it was yesterday. As has become the norm, I always have my trusty backpack holding my blanket, emergency ostomy supplies, medicine and a book to pass the time when necessary. So I plopped it down on the counter and took the report out of the front zipper. I laid it out by itself, sat at the kitchen table and anxiously waited for Renee to walk in. When she came around the corner, I just pointed at it and watched. She is medically trained, a lot smarter than me and I knew she wouldn't be as confused as a football bat like I was when Dr. Hardiman was reading it to me. I could see her eyes moving further and further down the page and began to hear her sobbing. I got up from the table, slowly walked over to her and had the most soul encompassing hug of my existence. I will never forget that day until the good Lord takes me home.

My next step was to have the stint they placed in my bladder during surgery removed. They originally asked me to come and have it removed in the clinic without anesthesia. Big mistake! Without being too specific on how this procedure is done, to say it was painful is an understatement. As a matter of fact, it was the most painful thing I have experienced in my life. Quite frankly, I can't figure out for the life of me, why they would ever ask anyone to do it that way. Needless to say, it didn't work out and the stint had to stay in for another week until they booked me an operating room. So the next week I headed right back to UAB and this time the procedure took a total of three minutes on the operating table. A much better experience except for the fact a nurse shoved a swab so far up my nose that my brain took a couple days to recover. The joys of COVID.

Just like you usually have to wait 6-8 weeks for surgery after you finish rounds of chemo, the same is true after surgery before you can start chemo again. I had three more rounds left before I could ring that bell. If you have never experienced that yourself, it's very hard to put into words. Every time I walked in that Cancer Center and made my way to my chair, there was that bell hanging on the wall. Shinny and gold, waiting to be rung. During my time there, I heard that sound only once but it was permanently etched in my brain and to be honest was very motivational. A part of you is very happy for that person ringing the bell but there is another part of you that is extremely jealous. Every day that rolled off that calendar was one day closer to closing a chapter that quite frankly at times seemed would never come. You have set backs and delays that are out of your control but just like I've told my players for years; "Control what you can control" so that's what kept me focused. Sometimes, I would even hear that bell in my sleep! I would awake out of a dead sleep and have to ask myself, was that real?

The day finally came and as I sat in my chair receiving that last round of chemo, my thoughts actually began racing back to when I first started and how scared I was. Not because it was going to hurt or side effects people told me about but was it going work? I thought about meeting these amazing ladies for the first time and how they would receive my, in your face type of personality. I thought about how much time was spent in the car riding to and from with my unbelievable support team. But most of all, I thought about what I wanted to say to everyone that supported me through this journey. What could I possibly say to articulate the love I had for so many? The only thing I could think of was to do a video, so at least people would have a chance to hopefully see the appreciation and pure joy on my face!

During this journey I never posted pictures or videos from the hospital or cancer center but I guess there is a first time for everything. Well, this chemo treatment seemed like it took forever and with each passing minute the anticipation became mind numbing. What was I going to say? As I walked in the hallway towards the ceremonial bell, the crowd began to grow because unbeknownst to me, Ashley had let everyone know what was going on. It wasn't the amount of people that made me anxious, it was the fact that I still didn't know what I was going to say. I am never at a loss for words. As I approached the bell, in my mind I thought I was going to ring that thing so hard it would fall off the wall but honestly as I began to read the inscription my thoughts totally changed. It reads, "Ring this bell, three times well to celebrate the day! This course is run, my treatment done and I am on my way!"

While I was reading, I began to feel a lot of guilt in that moment. There are almost 2 million people diagnosed with cancer a year just in the United States and thousands of them have to go through this journey alone. On top of that, some don't even survive treatment and if they do, it is a horrible experience on them mentally and physically. Why do I deserve such grace? The only reason I could come up with is that God had a plan for me and it was to use this as a platform to reach others. It was so much more emotional than I ever anticipated. After I finished crying like a baby, I said my goodbyes and headed out that door towards the next leg of this journey.

As we were on the way home, I sent a copy of the video to school so they could post it on our social media and before we got home there were already thousands of views. Kind of blew my mind actually and before the night was over there were around twenty thousand views. Without my knowledge, Brianna, my oldest posted it on Tik Tok (what is that) and within a few days in got over 3 million views and almost 700,000 likes. Now that doesn't really mean a whole lot to me (not a big social media guy) and probably not much to people reading this book but after my disbelief subsided, I embraced it because that meant God was sharing my story. No way does my story reach that many people, that fast, without some divine intervention!

My next step was radiation treatment. I had to spend a week in Birmingham and again because of COVID, no one could come with me to treatments. To add to the fun, I developed a blood clot that week also. Just another hurdle to jump amidst what seemed to be a never ending track meet. Fortunately for me it didn't cause a delay in treatment but I did have to deal with edema (swelling) in my right leg for a long time because of it. I also noticed when I got out of the bed, there would be hair all over the pillow and when I took a shower, it would come off in my hands when I was rinsing my hair. I thought it was strange that this didn't happen during all those months of prior chemo but it was just another example on a long list of things I had no control over.

One bright spot that week, besides meeting more wonderful people at the UAB radiation facility, was my youngest, Macie, coming up to spend the night with me. She was getting ready to start her senior year in high school and UAB was on her list of potential schools so after treatment, we toured the campus and went out to dinner. Of course, there was a nap in between but never the less, it was great daddy/daughter time! I can tell you this, in the course of a year between chemo and radiation, I probably got more sleep than I have my entire life. It sure felt like it anyway.

Because I developed a blood clot in July, that delayed my ileostomy reversal surgery until October. Three more months of acceptance for a situation that I wanted no part of. There again, it came down to surrendering to God's will. He didn't bring me this far to abandon me now. My job was not to second guess his timing but to get up every day and try to be an inspiration to others. So that's what I did, put it out of my mind and went to work. We planned the surgery during Fall Break in hopes of missing as little school as possible and we had an off week in football as well. I guess, I got spoiled not having a surgery since March because the week before, I really started getting nervous. I don't know if nervous is the right word but I was definitely on edge. It wasn't that I didn't have faith in Dr. Hardiman or anything like that; I just don't like hospitals, I don't like being out of commission, I don't like depending on everyone (told you I was stubborn) and I really hate needles! You would think by now, I would be used to them but I'm not and never will be.

Unlike my surgery during the height of COVID, Renee was able to come with me this time and boy was I glad because it wasn't a very pleasant four days we were there. We went up the night before because the surgery was scheduled for 5:00 a.m. We had a nice dinner and just talked about being ready for all this to be over with. While at dinner, I started getting all these texts from random numbers that I didn't have in my phone. "Praying for you coach. Hope everything goes well. Wishing you a speedy recovery." I had forgotten that Barry Dean was going to send out a message to the Coaches Association about my surgery. There had to be at least a hundred of them; short and sweet but then I got a really long one.

This coach went on to say how my speech at the AlaBCA Coaches Clinic was as powerful as he had heard since attending and how it really touched him. It made him finally go get a colonoscopy that he had delayed for years. I think that really put me at ease that night and was just another example in a long line of selfless acts that helped me through this journey.

Of course, Dr. Hardiman was a rock star and the surgery was a success. I did find out later, while I was in recovery, she met with Renee and told her the surgery went well but in typical Coach Fanning fashion; harder than usual! She did tell me that my last surgery was definitely one of her toughest ever and I told her that I always liked being ranked #1. Sometimes you just have to make light of the situation to keep your sanity because this time it felt like a game of "pin the tail on the donkey". So for three more days, they stuck me and stuck me and stuck me. They had to make sure my blood levels were right before they sent me home because of the previous blood clot. I know they were doing what was necessary but it still sucked.

I did have a two-inch deep open wound as a parting gift as well as two arms that were shredded with puncture holes but I also had a beautiful scar on my chest; she removed my chemo port as well. It may seem a little odd that my description of a scar includes the word "beautiful" but that's what I saw. I saw only a reminder of how far I had come in a year in a half and how blessed I felt to even be walking out of that hospital. Yes, I had been through a lot and yes, I have a lot of permanent scars and a colostomy bag but that's not what I see when I look in the mirror. I see a walking, talking miracle. Those scars are battle wounds that allow me to tell a story. A story of how God put his heavenly armor around me, brought me through the wilderness, protected me from the evil that lies in wait for all of us and warmed my soul with a light that will sustain me for the rest of my days.

Obviously, I wouldn't wish this turn of events on anyone because of what this dreaded disease takes from you and most of all, how it attempts to drain the life out of the ones closest to you but that's only if you let it. I remember having to take Brianna to college the day after I was diagnosed and it was one of the most peaceful days of my life. Now, on the surface, you would think the exact opposite, right? Well, that day was the first day in probably 25 years that I didn't care what was on the to-do list, what I was going to eat, what time I had to leave or what crazy scheme my brain was trying to formulate to have the perfect life. I was only there to share in her moment, hug her as much as possible and try to burn every minute into memory. Like most of us, I had been taking those moments for granted for way too long.

Now every type of cancer is different and every treatment protocol differs from patient to patient. It depends on the type, what stage, your overall health and basically how much treatment you can withstand. Some require one surgery, some require several surgeries and some may even require no surgery. I do know this, just like mental toughness gives you an edge at your job, in your marriage, raising your children and even your walk with Christ;

the same is true when battling for your life. It's not ok to just accept it! It's not ok to just roll over! It's not ok to give in! Just like this disease, you have to be Relentless!

"Relentless in Christ and Relentless in your Life!"

CHAPTER 2
ANGELS ON EARTH

I have always considered myself superstitious but probably because of athletics more than anything. Always put your uniform on the same way every time, lucky batting gloves, a certain pair of sunglasses or even a picture or quote you keep tucked away in your hat. I have worn the same socks for eight straight years. Luckily for me, God blessed me with feet that don't stink. Now you can't convince new players on the team of that until they smell them! Pre-game routines are like the ten commandments for athletes. I can't tell you how many times I have told someone, "You know how many wins are in that; lucky rake, ball bucket, shop vac that we use to get water off the field and especially the ole fungo bat." The point is, you can insert a hundred things into that statement and they would all be true in my warped coaches' mind. We are definitely creatures of habit so when things start happening to you on a regular basis that are out of the norm, your antenna tends to go up.

For me it started about six months before I got diagnosed with cancer. It seemed like at least 3-4 times a week I would pull my phone out of pocket and it would be 3:33. For about a month I just chalked it up to being a creature of habit and for some reason I was just pulling my phone out of my pocket at the same time because of muscle memory. Then it started happening in my truck. I would look down at how many miles were left until my gas tank was empty (333). Football and basketball games seemed to always read 3:33 left in the half or quarter when I looked. It was on my stove clock when I walked through the kitchen. When I charged my watch and it came back on, you guessed it (3:33)! I started to tell my other coaches because I wanted to make sure I wasn't going crazy and every one of them said, "that means something, I don't know what but it has to mean something".

So what does anyone do when they don't know the answer, turn to Google of course! This is what I found. The spiritual meaning of 333: "Seeing the angel number 333 everywhere around you means that you're fully protected by divine beings from higher realms". Another website said, "The angel number 333 is a reminder from the angels that they are with you as you go through life's obstacles, guiding you and protecting you". After reading that, it made sense to me. I have always believed angels were watching over me. The places I've lived, the things I've witnessed and situations I have been in are mind blowing when I think about them sometimes. There is certainly no way to explain why I am still alive if not for their protection.

But why now? Why am I seeing these numbers all of a sudden? What are they protecting me from now? After a few months, I didn't pay too much attention to it anymore, even though it was still happening with regularity until. I was very fortunate to be able to take Macie to a Duke/North Carolina basketball game at

Duke and if you follow the sport at all, you know that's the holy grail of basketball events. Admittedly, I am a little biased but my brother-in-law, Ron Groover, is the best official in the country and he was calling the game. Macie and I toured the campus during the day; it has been a dream school of hers for a long time. The electricity around the arena was so cool. College Game Day was there of course and the Cameron Crazies were in full effect. Well the game itself may be remembered forever but not because it was an "instant classic" but because Zion Williamson blew out his shoe in the first minute of the game and never returned to the court. Well after settling my daughter down for being so angry, we still enjoyed the atmosphere, the competition and just the mystic of one of the greatest rivalries in the history of collegiate athletics. You can't really even sit down during breaks in the action or TV timeouts because it's so packed but the one thing I will never forget is looking up at the huge clock hanging over the court during a stop in play and you guessed it: 3:33. I still have the picture to this day.

It was so hard for me to make sense of the whole thing. It just felt like a normal Spring coaching baseball and I was planning our mission trips for the Summer like always (Puerto Rico & Dominican Republic). Like I alluded to earlier, there were some changes physically but I chalked that up to old age! Of course, hind sight being 20/20, now I know what these angels were telling me. I was just too stubborn to listen. Another angel I found on earth also became a fixture in my life on a daily basis. As a matter of fact, this angel came to see me twice a day, rain or shine.

This started almost to the day when I was diagnosed. I started hearing a loud tapping on the large window in the dining room early one morning so I went to investigate. I thought it might be a tree limb that had gotten too long but to my surprise it was a beautiful, bright red cardinal, just a pecking away. So I went back to the bedroom to get my wife and show her. Of course, by the time she got back out there with me, it was gone. Wouldn't you know that evening, it happened again. I kid you not, that bird showed up day after day after day at that window without fail each morning and each evening. On top of that, if we were out back on the deck, he would always come to perch in one tree in the morning and another three on the other side of the yard in the evening to talk to us. His sound was so calming and peaceful so I would whistle right back at him. I think God made me a great whistler because I can't sing a lick!

After realizing just how inspirational and definitely needed this little bird was in my life at the time, I found myself looking forward to seeing him each and every morning I got up. I would ask my wife sometimes, "have you heard him yet"? I wanted to make sure I didn't miss him because he always started my day off right. It didn't matter if I had chemo, a doctor's appointment or leaving for surgery, I wanted to see him before I left the house because I knew everything was going to be alright that day! I even thought about him when I was in the hospital recovering from surgeries. I thought to myself, will he still be there when I get home? And he was there every time for a year straight until the day I returned from radiation, he was gone! I checked for several days in a row and not a peep. I even found myself searching the yard, making my normal cardinal calls but nothing. After sitting on the back porch staring at the trees for about an hour, it finally dawned on me, his job was done!

Well, as I explained in the previous chapter, I went several months without being on chemo and without a surgery because of my blood clot. I was feeling good, somewhat normal I would say, so the smart money would have been to say the angels had done their job, right? Nope, as soon as I returned from the hospital after my last surgery, my beautiful cardinal returned and was there every day during my recovery. On top of that, Renee called me into the kitchen on Saturday morning while she was paying bills and just wanted to show me something on our credit card statement. Not that unusual of an ask, so I bee bopped in there and highlighted on the top of the statement (Medical - $333.33). I will give you one even better, as I was writing this, she sent me a snapshot of her phone screen that shows the number of emails she had. Just guessed it, bright red number, 333! Now it was happening to her.

I wouldn't be able to look myself in the mirror if I didn't mention to you the most important angel of all, my wife. No way I would have made it through this ordeal without her. She has comforted me, loved on me, changed my ostomy bags, tended to my wounds, made sure I took my medicine, helped me get dressed, and never batted an eye. You name it, she has done it. She is an amazing person with a heart of gold and God knew what he was doing when he put her in charge. There aren't wings or a halo big enough to fit around her presence in my life.

See, God plants angels in our lives for a reason, because we need them. Now often times we are too hard headed to realize it but trust me, he does. He knows what we can take and he knows when we need a little boost. He knew when I needed a random phone call from a former teammate I haven't spoken with in years. A text message from a former player just asking how I was doing. An email from a college coach from half way across the country I haven't seen or heard from in eons. I can't count the number of times I showed up at school down and out for whatever reason but I never left there that way.

God sent angels to me on a daily basis, except they didn't look like what you see in the movies or romanticize about when reading the bible. They didn't have wings or halos but what they did have was a purpose from on high. They were teachers, students, administrators, secretaries and janitors. When you add to that my inner-circle, I was surrounded everyday by angels. These people have no idea what an impact they had on my life when I needed it the most nor at the time did they even realize the magnitude of their simple actions. See when God uses us as a vessel to positively impact others in sometimes even profound ways, we don't even give it a second thought. You want to know why? Because, it's not us, its him! I know I would not be writing this right now if it was not his will that I do so.

All throughout time we have heard of miraculous healings, near death experiences and even physical feats that are unexplainable. That is, if you are a non-believer. I believe that anything is possible if you put your trust in the almighty. His heavenly angels come in so many forms, we just have to be in the right frame of mind to receive them.

"If you are not ready to see his Angels on Earth, they will fly right by!"

CHAPTER 3
LIFE OF SERVICE

Sir Winston Churchill once said, "We make a living by what we get, we make a life by what we give"!

A life of service is anything but easy, and it requires constant sacrifice. It is also hard to identify sometimes, simply because the results are often miles or even years away. The forks in the road are often very similar in an appearance and it becomes hard to choose which one to take. Therefore, service requires faith! Faith is exactly that and it requires us to open our hearts and minds to some things that may be uncomfortable at times but extremely necessary. If we knew the results, it wouldn't require us to step out of our comfort zone and show complete vulnerability.

Not everyone believes they are being called to a life of service but if we are believers in Jesus Christ, it is the life he has blessed us with. Serving others doesn't have to be flashy, and most often it only involves investing our time and opening our hearts. Our eyes are blinded to these opportunities quite frequently because we are looking to move on as quickly as possible. In our fast-paced society there is always something else on the to-do list that day.

Many of us work fifty, sixty, or even seventy hours a week and how many times have you heard someone say that there are not enough hours in a day? A lot, I would imagine. We hear it all the time because it runs through everyone's brain. I know many times as I reflect on the day late at night, I ask myself, *Did I miss an opportunity to invest in someone other than myself today?* Often the answer is yes.

Unfortunately, we cannot go back and say good morning to that person we walked right by or just go back and ask the person how his or her day is going. If you never ask, there is no opportunity to shed the smallest ray of light into a person's life who may desperately need it. So often we walk around in our little bubble and never open our eyes to see what is going on. You have no idea if someone is in an abusive relationship, just lost a loved one, is fighting an addiction or is just struggling with their spirituality. To be a positive influence for someone battling those things, it takes an investment of time.

Teachers and coaches have the greatest opportunity to be servants than in any other profession, and this is simply because they have a captive audience for about eight hours a day and when it comes to coaches, sometimes about twelve hours a day. What better platform can there be when young men and women are being shaped and molded into the people they will become for the rest of their lives. Dr. Billy Graham was quoted as saying, "One coach will impact more young people in one year than the average person does in a lifetime."

It is an enormous responsibility with big consequences but with even greater rewards! Look at the first true teacher to ever walk the face of the earth, Jesus. He led by example every day. He poured himself into others so they would in turn do the same. He knew his days were numbered so he paid the ultimate sacrifice and served until his last breath. Over two thousand years later, his service inspires, comforts and leaves an unshakeable example to follow.

Not everyone will choose a career that involves teaching and coaching young men and women. The United States Armed Forces is as good an example of serving something bigger than yourself that you can find in the world today. These professions are vitally important to the moral fabric of our society but it is so important to understand that anyone can lead a life of service.

I had a Little League coach (that I wrote about earlier) who invested so much in me, and I only hope he feels rewarded by the man I strive to be every day. I grew up without a father, so he was the first male role model I had when I could understand what that meant. He had a huge effect on my life, and his actions allowed me to see that there were people willing to help with no strings attached. There was only one reason for this grace he showed to me--he had a servant's heart! That was never more evident than when he showed up 35 years later to show his support for me on that football field. There are youth coaches all over the country who provide this type of leadership on a daily basis. Most often, they do not realize the positive influence of their actions until many years later.

What if Jesus would have sat on the sidelines? He could have watched as men and women morally destroyed themselves, but he didn't. He chose a life of service, and we should be eternally grateful. Yes, his act of service to humankind is unmatched but his everyday acts of kindness give us a blueprint for serving others. I have seen firsthand the effect that Habitat for Humanity can have on a family's life. Volunteering at a soup kitchen, at a battered women's shelter, or at your church, or even just donating clothes to Goodwill are all great opportunities to help. There are countless organizations that can and will always need help.

I would recommend that everyone at some point in time, if physically able, should go on a mission trip. It will change your life forever. If for nothing else, it will give you a greater appreciation for the life God has blessed you with. It's not possible to give that much of yourself and not feel its effects immediately. Remember though, putting a smile on someone's face at a homeless shelter for even the briefest of moments may make all the difference in the world. Hammering those nails on a roof that provides safety and shelter to someone who has experienced only personal tragedy can change a person's life forever. That's what servants do. Philippians 2:3-4 tells us, "Do nothing out of rivalry or conceit, but in humility consider others as more important than yourselves. Everyone should look out not only for his own interests, but also for the interests of others" (Holman Christian Standard Bible).

This holds true on a daily basis at work as well. If you have been blessed with a position of leadership, it is imperative that those looking to you for guidance and leadership see servant qualities. The most influential leaders over the course of time have inspired people through leading a life of service (Mother Teresa, Gandhi, and Martin Luther King Jr.). Leading with fear or a strong-arm approach will only last so long, because eventually those who work for you see it as exactly that. They should feel as though they are working with you instead of for you. They may begin to have no reservations about clocking out as quickly as possible without being penalized. However, if they feel you are emotionally invested in them as individuals and that you treat them with respect, they will usually follow you anywhere. This takes an investment of time. A servant-leader has no problem getting to know an employee's family, his or her likes and dislikes, his or her favorite sports teams, where the employee attends church, or if he or she likes to travel. This means it is about serving something bigger than yourself and not the bottom line. The goal of every leader should be to build other great leaders. You should lead employees as if they would eventually take your job. Leaders that only use fear and scare tactics are most often masking insecurities about their personal lives, professions, or spirituality.

It doesn't matter if you are a Republican or a Democrat. It doesn't matter if you are Catholic or Assemblies of God. It doesn't matter if you are a world class athlete, a complete nerd or even both. It doesn't matter if you are a super-model or have one tooth. It doesn't matter if you are a millionaire or struggle to make ends meet. It doesn't matter what color your skin is. It doesn't matter where you were born. What does matter? None of these things I just listed, prevent any of us from being nice to each other. Quit worrying about what you see on TV, search your heart for guidance and I promise you will have a peace you didn't know existed. We allow so much garbage into our brains and if we would just take out the trash, our lives would be so much different. We all have to ability to serve others!

This is the case for education, military service, politics, manufacturing or raising a family. Being the leader of your family is more important than any job title you could possibly obtain. Children love unconditionally, and it slowly slips away as the world weighs on them. They are blinded by expectations not only by their peers but also by their parents. Take them with you when volunteering. Let them see the influence one person or a group of people can have on the world. If children are shown examples of kindness by serving others, there is a good chance as they grow and mature, they too will choose this path because it is already ingrained in them. Today, so many of us find ourselves worrying about how much money we earn, how big our houses are or how good our clothes look. I am going let you in on a little secret--we can't take any of those things with us! I heard Denzel Washington say during a speech one time, "I have never seen a U-Haul attached to a hearse!" The only thing we have with us as we stand before God is our salvation. What have we done to further his kingdom on earth?

"Have we given to others as his son has given to us?"

CHAPTER 4
GOD'S PATH

I think most children grow up and think they are destined for greatness at some point. Everyone wants to be a "superstar" right? So what does that mean? Well if we watch television that probably means a professional athlete, an actor, politician or a CEO of a Fortune 500 company. That couldn't be further from the truth. We think these things signify greatness because that's what society tells us. Very seldom do you see a janitor on television that has worked for 30 years at the same school and changed countless lives during that time, simply because they always put the kids before themselves. He or she merely shared a kind word when they showed up to work before anyone else or stayed after everyone else has gone home for the evening. That lonely kid sitting on the sidewalk only needed an investment of time to make all the difference in the world. Maybe that janitor is the example this young man or woman needed to show them accountability, kindness and that it doesn't matter what the time clock says. God has a path for all of us. Maybe that path is that of a professional athlete, a lawyer, a doctor or a mechanic, it is really irrelevant.

Sometimes and quite frankly most times that path is hard to see. There are many twists, turns, peaks and valleys but rest assure it is right there in front of you. It takes prayer and a lot of faith.

But faith in its self is difficult for many of us because we want the answers to the test. One of my favorite lines in a movie is by Tom Hanks in *A League of Their Own*. His star player is about to quit the team because it just got too hard and his response was, "If it wasn't hard everyone would do it, the hard is what makes it great!" The same is true during our walk on God's Path; the decisions are often difficult because we don't see the results immediately.

I would encourage everyone to do an exercise as you read this. Take a piece of paper and chronological begin to write as a diagram your path so far in life. Starting from where you were born and ending where you currently reside today. In between those, begin to fill in your stops along the way. This would include but not limited to college choices, jobs you have taken, churches you have attended or even how you met your significant other. There are no limits to this, include as much as you want because you will be blown away by what you find. Some of the smallest details in your life, God put there and some would define these as "divine appointments". As you think about these significant milestones in your life, reflect back and ask what nudged you one way or the other. Why did I choose this direction instead of another? Did I pray when making these decisions? Whom did I seek advice from during this time? As a child these paths are most often determined by our parents but their decisions are extremely influential in our decision making process as we get older. Parents are the first examples we have. Their lives unfold right in front of us and we steadily catalog these things in our minds even if we do it unknowingly. Teachers, coaches, pastors or even older siblings are more examples of influential people that help us shape our perspective while choosing a path in life. One of the greatest gifts God bestowed upon us is the power of choice!

As I have asked each of you to examine God's Path for your life, I will do the same. My mother was born in Foxboro, Massachusetts. She chose a life of service by enlisting in the United States Army to be a nurse which led her to be stationed in Fort Benning, Georgia. Shortly thereafter, she had me out of wed-lock and decided to keep me instead of giving me up for adoption. This meant she would be discharged. This was not a popular decision with her family so we settled in Columbus, GA which was just outside the base. Until I was nine we lived in South Columbus and then we moved to East Columbus across from Eastern Little League and the Boy's Club. As I look back, I know God led my mother here. That little league coach I mentioned earlier, Gary Reuseski, this is where our paths crossed. It was my first experience with organized sports and it was definitely what I needed to keep me focused and out of trouble. Not to mention I had access to the Boy's Club every day after school which was a blessing for a single mother not to have to worry where I was. This was also about the same time we changed churches and I began to develop a personal relationship with Christ. Several years later as high school was quickly approaching, my mother moved us to North Columbus where I attended Jordan High School.

In high school, my paths crossed with Coach Fred Maynard and Coach Paul Waldrop. Coach Maynard was young and just out of college. He treated me like a little brother which included kicking me in the butt on occasion to keep me on the straight and narrow in the classroom. He really invested time in me when he wasn't on the clock, which included after school pick-up basketball games and just talking about life in general. I can still see those rec-specs he wore like it was yesterday. Coach Waldrop was a seasoned veteran and really challenged me as an athlete. He made me realize that playing college athletics was a realistic goal. He was a disciplinarian in ever since of the word and held everyone accountable for their actions. Not to mention buying me my letterman jacket because my mother couldn't afford one. How would my life have turned out if these men wouldn't have chosen a life of service? I decided to attend Berry College on a baseball scholarship. The decision wasn't easy but I felt its academic reputation and beautiful campus in the North Georgia Mountains put it over the top for me.

After only one semester in college, I found myself at a crossroads. The coach that recruited me was leaving to take another job and I just felt like I was being led in another direction. I had friends from high school playing baseball at Middle Georgia College in Cochran, GA. Like the reputation Berry College built academically, MGC had built a reputation for nationally ranked junior college teams and producing professional baseball players. So how would I get there? Well, I didn't have a car so I had to talk a teammate in to taking me 3 hours south and even then I had no idea if the legendary Coach Robert Sapp would even take me. I showed up, glove in hand and asked for a tryout. I don't know if he saw something in me or just felt sorry for me but I know God had a plan. What do you know, the friends I knew from high school left before I started the next semester and the teammate that took me all the way down there, Rusty Evans, is still a friend of mine to this day. He is an Athletic Director at a school that we compete against and even had me come speak to a group of Athletic Directors at a clinic they were hosting.

Almost a year after I made that big decision as I was eating in the cafeteria, in walked my future wife. I chased her down the hall like a stalker and the rest they say is history. That was 28 years ago and we have two beautiful daughters because of it. What is unfortunate is that so many people will say, man that is ironic. There is nothing ironic about it, God's Path put me in that exact place at that exact time and he gave me the strength to act. How many times in life do we want to go back in time and try to play Monday morning quarterback, that only leads to the biggest regrets in our lives. I could have just as easily become stricken with the fear of rejection but that's what Faith is all about! Six months later, I was faced with another life altering decision on where to go after junior college.

I was so blessed to have several scholarship offers to great four-year schools but up until this point in my life, it was still the hardest decision by far. On paper, it seemed like an easy decision to stay closer to home but in the end I chose Marshall University, which geographically made the least amount of sense being over eight hours away. When I visited, something in my gut felt right even though I knew it would put a tremendous strain on my relationship with Renee and I would only get to come home twice a year. It was extremely hard in many ways but I would find out years later why God's Path led me there.

After I was done playing college baseball, I signed a two-year, independent minor league contract to play for the Portsmouth Explorers of the Frontier League. During the off-season I got a job at Neil's Sports Shop and took a few classes to finish up my degree. Not long after, another big decision in my life was about to unfold. I was given the opportunity to travel around the entire country for three months with the Olympic Torch Relay. The company I was working for had secured the merchandising rights and was putting together a team to do mobile merchandise that started in Los Angeles and would finish in Atlanta for the start of the 1996 Olympic Games. So what was God's Path? If I took this opportunity, it was almost certain my baseball career would be over, not to mention I would be away from my fiancée for three months. Over the past four years, we had been apart for nearly half of it but after weighing the options, I decided to go. As I look back on this part of my life, sometimes I wonder if I had to do it all over again would I make the same decision? All of our lives are filled with these moments and that is why "faith" is such an integral part of the path we choose.

It really was the experience of a lifetime up until that point in my life. I had never traveled anywhere baseball had not taken me, so seeing so much beauty really opened my eyes to a world I didn't know existed. From flower farms in the Pacific Northwest to the breathtaking Rocky Mountains; the start of the Mississippi River in Minnesota to where it ends in New Orleans; the beginning of the Erie Canal and Niagara Falls to the swamps of South Florida. Of course, I also didn't mind meeting Rick Pitino in Louisville and Bill Russell in Seattle or getting to run the Olympic Torch close to my home town as my mom looked on. But only until after this wonderful experience was over, did I truly understand why this path was there for me. The company I was working for offered me a full-time job and that allowed me to close the baseball chapter of my life and legitimately look towards marriage.

Over the next three years I would travel all over the world managing merchandise venues at sporting events. We went to Japan for the Winter Olympics, France for World Cup Soccer, worked two Super Bowls and did all the SEC and Big East Championship games. I was in my early twenties, standing on the sidelines of an SEC Football Championship game, sitting on the first row in Madison Square Garden for the Big East Championship Game right behind legendary Syracuse coach Jim Boeheim and I even got to meet Mahammad Ali at an event we did. What a blessing, it was high intensity, constant problem solving and being around some of the biggest sporting events in the world. It helped fill a void in my life now that college athletics were a thing of the past. Renee and I were married in May of 1997 and my trip to Japan was in January of 1998. It was tough going away for almost a month as a newly-wed but wouldn't you know, the first person that walked in our venue when we opened the doors, I knew from the torch relay. Now that's a "divine appointment"! Our lives are littered with God's subtle touches like that, knowing what we need and when we need it.

Little did I know around the corner would be a life changing decision. The company I was working for bought back The Game Headwear Company and my job responsibilities changed. After a while in my new assignment, I knew deep down in my heart, this was not my calling. When you go from a position that's so fast paced and constantly changes at the drop of a hat to a more traditional 9 to 5 environment, it shocks the system. I was used to working 100-hour work weeks at an event, traveling to places I had never been before and just the electricity that accompanied special events was hard to replace. It was a great company and my bosses were great people. They had given me the opportunity to travel around the world and in a lot of ways helped shape my perspective on life. Again, several years later I would understand exactly why God allowed me this opportunity and how important it would be to his path for the rest of my life.

As I began searching for answers on pretty much a daily basis, a friend of mine called me about a teaching and coaching position at Glenwood School. Glenwood is a small private school in Phenix City, Alabama. I grew up in public school education however, during high school I had friends from summer baseball that went to school there so I had heard about it. After discussing it with my wife, I went for an interview and realized very quickly it was a something I wanted to do. Now wanting to do something and having the courage to actually do it are two very different things entirely. First, I had to go home and tell my wife what the contract offer was and that it would be a significant pay cut. Second, she was right in the middle of getting her Masters of Physical Therapy at the Medical College of Georgia which was being done at a satellite campus an hour and half a way from where we lived already. Third, there would be a lot of Ramen noodles on the menu until she graduated.

Of course, Renee has always supported everything I have ever done so the newest chapter of my life had begun. Not only was our headmaster a great leader, I also had the privilege of working for two of the greatest coaches in Alabama history (Coaching Coaches chapter). Our football coach, Wayne Trawick, is the 2nd winningest coach in Alabama high school history and our basketball coach/athletic director, Doug Key, is the 2nd winningest coach in Alabama Junior College history. They have been elected to numerous halls of fames and these are the men that God placed in my life to spend time with on a daily basis. The first two things I noticed was how humble they were and how they treated everyone. They have no idea what an impact that made on me as a young man searching for inspiration.

It wasn't very long into my coaching career when I knew I could make a difference in the lives of young men and women. Earlier in this chapter when I said it would be years later before I realized why I ended up at Marshall University, well here you go. Three years into coaching, one of my former players, Josh McConnell was playing baseball at Faulkner University and he called to tell me it wasn't working out. He was done with baseball. My response was no you're not, you are about to get in this truck with me and take a journey. I was getting ready to take two kids up to Marshall (8.5 hours away) for a camp and wouldn't you know he ended playing DI baseball for three years because of my relationship with that program. He even ended up going to Spain to play baseball, how cool is that? Josh also came back home after he was finished with school, coached with me for ten years and has since moved on to become a Head Coach and Athletic Director. He chose to invest in others the same way people had invested in him. It gets better, as I will soon explain. I want to stay chronologically on God's Path in my life for the sake of this chapter.

After four years of being an assistant coach in baseball, basketball and football, I was given the opportunity to be the head baseball coach in the spring of 2004 and Athletic Director in 2005. I only tell you this because choices needed to be made on how to run a baseball program and when there are choices to be made; God's Path comes in to play. The Glenwood baseball program is stepped in tradition; they had won 14 state championships in 34 years of existence but had not won a title since 1993. That just happened to coincide with long-time and celebrated major leaguer, Tim Hudson's, graduation. I had a vision and it required a lot of changes. Usually with change comes resistance and wouldn't you know, two of my former bosses at my previous job, had become two of my biggest supporters. Phil Stillwell was co-founder of The Game Headwear Company and Tommy Allison was a partner in their current business and both of their sons played for me. Even though you know what you doing is right, sometimes you still need that support system for encouragement when that self-doubt creeps in. You need someone to say, "Stay the course!" They are two of my very best friends still to this day. You think God put them on my Path for a reason?

I feel the next significant road on God's Path for me started in about 2011. We had just won a third consecutive state championship but I just felt more was needed from me as a servant. Mrs. Lynda Wright, a science teacher at our school, had been taking groups to Central America for about 15 years, for service trips during the summer. I would always talk to her about these trips when they returned and quite frankly I was very envious of their experiences. We would talk about how I need to take my players and teach kids baseball. Well, this summer when they returned Mrs. Wright told me she found the perfect place for us to start. Again, it is one thing to talk about something and something entirely different stepping up to the plate and doing it. I started praying about this a lot and sharing my thoughts with Coach McConnell. He suggested that I call Marshall Murray, his best friend from college. Marshall had started a non-profit organization called "More Than A Game". I met Marshall through Josh when they played together. Funny how Marshall University keeps popping up after a decision I made almost 30 years ago but that's how God's Path works. "More Than A Game" sponsored amateur teams in Northern California with an emphasis on serving their community through camps, equipment drives and local service projects. After talking with Marshall, I began to work on the blueprint for the International Missions side of "More Than A Game." In October of 2012, we took our first trip to the village of Bongo in the Northern Province of Panama. Since then, we have been back to Panama twice, Cameroon (Africa), Colombia (South America) three times, the Dominican Republic several times, Costa Rica, Taiwan, Puerto Rico and have also done amazing things domestically all over the country.

I always felt drawn to a life of service but as you make your way through life, sometimes the corporate ladder seems more attractive. Well, like a lot of people you don't realize how long that ladder is and what you may have to give up, to reach the top. I don't just mean giving up time but giving up who you really are and what truly makes you happy. Of course, I had no idea God's Path for me would have included cancer but now that it has, my perspective on life has changed so much.

Recognizing that each little special moment in our lives is there for a reason is hard for us to digest. Most of the time it escapes us because it's so much bigger than our brain can wrap itself around. It's not until we gain some perspective, possibly due to age or even life events that we can truly see the big picture. I can tell you this with a 100% certainty, there is no way in the world, I make it through the last year and a half of my life without God's Path being laid out for me. The plan for my life was pre-ordained by the holy of holies and thank goodness because he is a whole lot smarter than I will ever attempt to be. What I hope for everyone is that they don't look back 20 years from now and say, what could I have done different? Should I have recognized the signs? Was I too scared to trust my heart?

"So you have to ask yourself, are you on God's Path or your own?"

CHAPTER 5
PANAMA

For the most part people want to be good. I bet if you ask 100 people, 95 of them would tell you that they always wanted to go on a mission trip but just never have. When the opportunity arose and the invitation was extended, suddenly the laundry list of reasons why they couldn't go started piling up: Finances, Work, Kids, Illness, Lack of travel experience, Fear of the region traveling to. This is very common when anyone attempts to step out of their comfort zone because of uncertainty. It is natural for us to second guess, rationalize and experience fear when it comes to matters of the heart. If you can ever overcome that fear and merely just give your heart a chance, it will allow your hands to touch so many. I have personally witnessed the transformation in people when they just let go and commit. The only way I know how to explain it is that it's like watching the curtain rise at a play and seeing a whole new world you never noticed before. Then you start thinking, this has been right in front of me and I have never taken a moment to open my eyes and see it. It's so fulfilling to watch people experience this because it is truly life-changing. Colors are brighter, sounds are sharper and even smells are more magnified. The old saying, "It's like a kid in a candy store!"

This is a good opportunity to tell you about the fore-mentioned mission trips and the impact they have had not only on my life but countless others. The thing about organizing mission trips is that you can prepare all you want, do all the research your brain can handle and the reality is when you have boots on the ground; expect the unexpected! Prepare to be disappointed at times and at the same time have your heart melt like butter. One thing I have learned without a shadow of a doubt, never expect to be on time! It is extremely hard for us to comprehend this because the society we live in is totally built on schedules. A lot of our lives revolve around being at work at a certain time, taking a lunch break at a certain time or being at an event at a certain time. In most countries, that is abnormal instead of the norm. Everything moves at a much slower pace and the sooner you come to grips with that, the more you can accomplish and better yet appreciate.

Our first trip was to Bongo, Panama. It is located about 20 miles from the border of Costa Rica at the base of Volcan Baru. We flew into Panama City, spent the night in a hotel and up at 4:00 a.m. to catch a small commuter plane to David, Panama. Seeing the expressions on the kid's faces when that plane taxied up with twin engine propellers was priceless. It probably didn't help the anxiety level very much when at the ticket counter the attendant asked everyone their weight. One of the best things about stepping out of your comfort zone is being able to share all these once and a lifetime experiences with others. We were the last people to get on the plane because I wanted to video everyone getting on together and we soon realized that having a sit assignment on your ticket didn't really mean anything. The flight was completely full so we took the only seats available. I was the very last person to get on and just like we discussed earlier, God's Path was laid out for me. This time it was about four feet wide and had running lights directly to where I was supposed to be at that moment in my life. I sat down next to an older gentleman. He looked like he was straight out of a Panama Jack commercial; tan, white linen pants, black silk shirt and white hat. His name was Frank Melgar, he just fell in love with our kids and was so appreciative of the mission we were on. He was very adamant about helping us with any future trips we wanted to take involving the kids of Panama. I would later learn just how serious he was about that proposition.

After we landed, white knuckles and all, it was time to rent our van and begin a rather tedious thirty-minute drive that turned into two and half hours. Little did we know that on this day there would be protestors blocking the main road to our destination so it was "figure it out" mode. But like always, God knew what he had planned for us because our journey was through some of the most beautiful countryside I have ever seen. When we finally turned on to that gravel road, it was like going through a porthole to another dimension. We had to cross a one lane bridge over this gorgeous river and when I saw a man riding on a horse, I figured it would be different than what we were used to. We stayed with a retired Methodist Minister, Secundino Morales and his wife Vicky. It seemed like every inch of this village was covered with some sort of crops. The air was filled with the smell of citrus because everywhere you walked there were oranges and limes just lying on the ground.

Our goal was to work with two small schools in the village on basic baseball fundamentals, supply them with equipment and uniforms and also leave them FCA Bibles printed in Spanish. After talking with Secundino, we learned that two elderly people in the village needed vegetable gardens built so we immediately added that to the list of priorities.

After surveying the village, we quickly realized that finding somewhere flat to do a baseball clinic was impossible so we used a small piece of uneven, rocky land in front of one of the schools until we could come up with an alternative solution. So we broke out all the bat bags full of equipment and set up a throwing, fielding and even a hitting station up against an old hog wire fence. It really didn't matter where we were; all that mattered is that every boy and girl had a smile on their face. During the hitting station, one of the boys hit the ball into the jungle and came back with an orange instead. Well, they decided to hit that too! In the throwing station, one boy looked like he was pitching the 7th game of the World Series he was so serious and focused. It was an amazing day. The next day we found a field about twenty minutes away but the problem was transporting everyone there. With Secundino's help, we had small pick-up trucks loaded with as many kids as possible. We had to use unpaved roads at very slow speeds but eventually we were playing baseball in Concepcion. All the kids played in their school uniforms, boys in dress pants and the girls in dresses. Again, it didn't matter, all smiles! As soon as the trucks stopped, these kids sprinted to the field and were racing each other around the bases in 95-degree weather. Little things like this seem to make a huge impact on our team. At home it is easy to take for granted having a uniform, equipment and a place to play. The kids from Bongo had none of these things. They walk jungle paths to school, many of them live on dirt floors, they eat to sustain life not for self-satisfaction and they were as happy as any kids I've ever seen. The next day we pulled out uniforms and hats to give all the kids; we might as well have been wearing Santa Claus outfits and passing out I-phones.

When we were done with baseball for the day, we bought all of the children drinks at the corner store. They were ice cold glass bottles of peach, strawberry, apple and orange soft drinks that cost 40 cents each. After that, we were working on vegetable gardens each day. Of course we had no idea what building a vegetable garden in Bongo, Panama actually entailed, but it was interesting to say the least. We did quickly figure out why we needed to do baseball in the mornings because every afternoon the rain was definitely coming. At Daniel's house, we had to harvest bamboo, carry it about a mile through the jungle and the only tool we had in the arsenal was a machete. It was definitely a more comprehensive job than we anticipated so it took about four afternoons to finish but in the end I think everyone was extremely proud of their work.

Each day we finished, the team went for a refreshing swim in the local river; it was cold and crystal clear. It was a short hike after crawling under a fence and it seemed as if we were transported to Jurassic Park. The river was surrounded with tall cliffs that were covered as far as the eye could see with massive ferns. The sun could barely break through the thick jungle canopy so there were areas of beautiful shadows and very brief moments of sparkling sunlight off the rocky rapids. We did some rock surfing and even created our own spa; equipped with a homemade Jacuzzi created by the current from the top of the rocks. People back in the states spend several hundred dollars for this kind of relaxation therapy.

Another early morning started at 4:30 a.m. for our epic journey to the top of Vulcan Baru (11,400 feet), the highest point in the country of Panama. We had about an hour drive before we started hiking. We met our two guides, Genover and Carlos at the base of the volcano. I had heard stories of how hard this adventure would be and in some opinions was an impossible task for a group this size. Altitude sickness and physical exhaustion were the two main concerns but I believe it was that chance of impossibility that had our group so focused on making it. The hike started with dense jungle in the dark so everyone had their headlamps on. Even as hard as you could immediately tell it was going to be, it was like God created a stairway to heaven for us to make it. Perfectly placed rocks and roots made steps attainable. It even seemed as if vines and branches were readily available upon request to use as ladders. After about two hours in the jungle it began to clear a little and show more of the volcano's true nature. The next quadrant as we called it produced more rocks and narrow pathways. Each quadrant had slightly different vegetation but each one as beautiful as the next.

Our guides were great about stopping for breaks where we shared about the hike to that point, asked questions, and enjoyed some water or sandwiches made by Mrs. Morales. Each one of us had our own battle with the mountain. To the person, it was the hardest thing any of us had ever done. About six hours up, there were several of us questioning our judgment but when we reached the summit it was well worth it. I can't begin to explain how life changing and freeing that experience was. There was also an 8 foot cross constructed at exactly 11,400 feet; there was a gold medallion put on it by the government to solidify its importance. It took us about 7 hours to finally reach the top so a little rest and meditation time was required.

We all spread out; some took a nap, some just stared out over the valley below, some enjoyed a little water but I am quite sure all of us were processing random thoughts about what we had just accomplished. I took a moment by myself at the base of the cross to thank God for allowing me to be in that exact place in time and giving me the strength to do something so amazing. Before we began our trek down, I talked to the boys about what should follow by accomplishing a feat like this and that there is nothing in their lives too big for them to handle. This journey was only a microcosm of the obstacles they will surely face in life (God's Path, School, Marriage, Kids, Career, Etc.).

We took a different route down the mountain and it was more in the shape of a very rocky road with ditches on both sides. After about 10 total hours of hiking, everyone was out of water. We were not in dyer straights by any means but that sure didn't seem to matter because another divine appointment was just around the corner. Just so happens on this occasion it was with a two-liter bottle of water. As I was walking, I saw what I thought was a big bottle of water on the edge of the jungle. So I walked past it back and forth for a few seconds, maybe thinking I was on candid camera but really thinking it might be boobie trapped. After a few more seconds of deliberation, I picked it up and noticed it had never been opened before; unbelievable! I gathered everyone, we all shared and no one certainly cared who they were drinking after.

It sure didn't take everyone very long to fall asleep that night. The next day we were going to visit the schools and present them with the FCA Bibles and some school supplies that local college students from our area had donated. The end of this trip was quickly approaching so everyone wanted to get one more swim in the river to put an exclamation point on our time in Bongo.

Little did we know it would be an adventure none of us would soon forget. It started off just like all the other days we went swimming. We were all spread out among the rapids in our little spas as we talked about the kids, Mrs. Morales' great food, hiking and how we would explain this experience to our friends and family when we returned home and all of a sudden we spotted a large log floating down the river. Not being from the mountains of Panama, it didn't seem that strange at first but in about five minutes we quickly realized what that floating log truly represented. Unbeknownst to us it had been raining in the mountains all day so the river was beginning to rise and to say we were unprepared is an understatement. Within minutes all of us were being over taken by raging waters. Decisions had to be made immediately! There were five us at the bottom of the rapids that had a fighting chance if there was no hesitation, so we went for it. As the stronger swimmers made it to the bank, they extended large branches to give assistance.

However, there were four people trapped in the river up above facing extreme decisions. I felt our best option for those guys was to stay put and work on a strategy for extraction. By this time, one young man lunged for the bank and crawled out through the jungle while the remaining three were above the water on large boulders. I didn't necessarily feel they would be swept away but amidst all this, darkness had fallen in the jungle. Cold, wet, pitch black darkness and a raging river in the jungle is a pretty good recipe for high levels of anxiety. I sent two boys back to the house to get a rope as we made our way back up river through some of the densest jungle I have ever seen. My goal while waiting for the rope to arrive was merely to calm any fears the guys may have had by just talking to them and letting them know what was going on. When the rope arrived, it wasn't heavy enough to throw across the water so we tied a rock to the end to gain distance. Secundino had a flash light behind me as I would make each toss and give me advice in his Panamanian James Earl Jones voice. Honestly it felt like instructions from heaven because of the deep voice and rays of light bouncing off the tress. It took about another hour but we finally were able to pull everyone out. It was definitely a trying moment and life lesson for all involved. When we finally made it back out to the road, with no shirts or shoes huddled up together, we asked Secundino to say a prayer and thank God for his protection in our time of need. So there we stood with no shirts, no shoes, soaking wet, shivering, holding hands and standing in a circle with only the head lights from the van illuminating a small area giving thanks. It was truly a sight to see and certainly something I will never forget as long as I live.

Our next trip to Panama was certainly less eventful but every bit as challenging. During our first trip we noticed the desire for playing the game of baseball was very real but the kids didn't have a place to play. We had to take them some 30 minutes away to find a field and for these families that was unrealistic moving forward. Many of them do not have cars so what could we do? Well we solicited corporate sponsors back in the states for the sole purpose of returning to build a baseball field in the jungles of Bongo. Getting all the necessary equipment on site to complete this mission was no small task I can assure you. Most of the roads surrounding this village are dirt or some form of gravel so getting heavy equipment to the field location was the first major hurdle or so we thought. When organizing trips like this, you are always looking for a way to trim costs to make the trip as affordable as possible. So in doing this, I mapped out an alternative route to Bongo through Costa Rica which would require us to rent a car and drive from San Jose. Well there was one problem with this great idea, unbeknownst to me, rental cars are not allowed across the border. So upon receiving this wonderful news standing at the rental car counter, there was only one option, hurry to the airport and pray there was a flight to David. Mind you, this flight only exists three days a week but as usual God was looking out for us and there was a flight leaving in an hour. Lost in all this was the fact that this extra flight was not in our budget and it was going to cost us over a $1,000 we did not have. So just like any other red blooded American would do, I charged it! Like so many other times in my life, I trusted God's Path and of course as you will see later in this chapter, he did not let us down.

Upon finally arriving in Bongo, we knew it was essential to clear and level this land before anything else could be done. Remember we are at the base of a volcano, so to tell you there were a lot of rocks is an understatement. Some of these rocks were over 400 pounds so moving them by hand was not an option. We had also arranged, with the help of Turface Athletics, for a container to be delivered with field maintenance products, rakes, bases, home plate, mound, etc.

Like I mentioned earlier, if you get too frustrated when things do not arrive in a timely fashion, you will walk around mad all the time. So while we waited for the equipment and container to show up, we started constructing a backstop out of bamboo. To my knowledge it had never been done before so we certainly didn't have a manual or prior experience to pull from. So we laid out the 60 x 20-foot net we dragged through customs in what looked like a body bag. You should have seen some of the looks we got in the airports and it was certainly a topic for discussion with several armed agents until they opened it. Even then, it was hard to explain what we were doing with it and where we were taking it. We cut the biggest bamboo we could find and dugs holes for support. Then we painted all the poles black and hung the net (it took three tries but it was finally up and functional). Because of the tropical environment and rainy season approaching we felt it was necessary to develop a drainage system around the field so we used a pick axe to hand dig a trench around the perimeter and filled it with rocks. We even cut bamboo to make foul poles and painted them yellow. After two days of this, the heavy equipment showed and we started moving some dirt. It was the darkest soil I had ever seen in my life. It certainly made sense after seeing this why almost every inch of land in this village had some sort of crops on it.

We leveled and picked up rocks for three days with the help of local villagers. We ran our strings, installed bases and a pitching rubber. Game on! When I tell you the people of Bongo came out to see their new field, I mean it. It was lined from one end of the field to the other. On the day before our departure, we played all day long. First, the kids played, then the women played and then the men played. Basically people were coming out of the jungle from all directions to see what this was all about. Unfortunately, like all trips, our time was up in this wonderful place but our team had one more stop before returning to the states. Remember Frank Melgar from our first trip to Panama, I called him Panama Jack. We were headed to see his place and take him up on his offer.

All we knew is the name of his resort, Pacific Bay Resort, and a general direction to go in from Bongo towards the coast. You have to understand there is no interstate system or reliable map to use. I remember on our first trip to Panama, Secundino got lost getting us to Bongo after detouring around the protest and he lives there. However, through email communication with Frank, I did have confidence we would get to the coast in close enough proximity to find it eventually. That uncertainty can be scary or very exciting depending on a person's perspective. Most of our lives are filled with certainty and not enough uncertainty. Uncertainty can cripple some and inspire others. It's all about your goals in life and what you strive to obtain from it. For me, I love surprises and going anywhere I have never been before. If I have never been there, there is a great chance I will experience and feel something I never have before. So many possible life-changing moments are missed every day because people are gripped with the fear of uncertainty.

After about a three-hour drive, we finally had no more land to drive on. We parked at a church and started asking around and the answers we got shocked us to say the least. Everyone we asked had the same answer, "You need a boat!" So we started asking local fishermen if they could take us and finally one agreed to the price we were able to pay. It's hard to describe the feeling heading out into the Pacific Ocean unsure of where you will end up, trusting in someone you've never met before and what lies around the next corner so to speak. So for about 45 minutes we just took in breath taking views of the sun setting over what seemed like hundreds of islands just of the coast. The boat begins to slow and the fisherman begins to point. We see a set of stairs heading up the steep face of this island. As we get closer, two men appear and begin walking towards the shore. It felt like we were on an episode of "Fantasy Island" except we were arriving in a boat and not "de plane". There was no dock so when the boat came to a halt, we had to take our shoes off and carry our luggage out over the water. I guess Frank forgot to mention that he owned an island.

The two guys waiting on the beach took us to the top of the island and showed us our rooms. We did immediately notice that there was no air conditioning and no television sets. Not exactly what most people from the states would call a resort but we soon figured out why it was precisely that. Frank had placed twelve of these rooms throughout the island, totally secluded from one another. There was a beautiful cove for kayaking and snorkeling on one side of the island. It even had hammocks nestled in the palm trees for a quick siesta. The other side of the island had a nice beach with a clear view of the ocean. The most impressive feature was the common eating area on the highest point of the island. Our dinner that first night was amazing and the view was literally inspiring. We talked about the trip and how blessed we were to be in this exact place at this exact time. What if we would have allowed our uncertainty to rule our decision in making this journey or not? It would have been much easier to stay in Bongo another day where we felt comfortable, get on a plane the next day and come back to our everyday lives. Look what we would have missed; a rare opportunity to look at the world through a different pair of glasses.

By the time we headed back to our rooms it was dark. When I mean dark, you couldn't see your hand in front of your face. As I described before there are no modern amenities so you lay in bed and just listen to the jungle. It's actually a great time to reflect on your life, think about your family and for me the legacy I strive to leave behind when I am gone. The next day we got up early to go explore the island. We saw howler monkeys, huge iguanas and gorgeous birds. As we trekked around the outside of the island, we found caves to hike through that had passage ways coming out the other side farther down the shoreline. Not until several hours later would we figure out why those holes existed. Like most of the islands in this region, they were shaped from volcanic activity so most of its formation is made of jagged black rock. After about three hours of hiking we figured it was time to head back so as not miss a nicely prepared meal from the Pacific Bay Resort staff. Well we waited just a little too long to head back because the tide had already started coming in. Those caves I spoke of earlier; they were completely filled with water. There were some dicey moments but thank the good Lord we made it back and learned another very valuable lesson when it comes to mother nature.

At lunch, Frank got on to us about leaving too many lights on the night before because everything on the island runs on solar power. When he was finished giving us a hard time, he asked if we wanted to go fishing and of course we said yes immediately. None of us had ever been fishing in the Pacific Ocean and I am pretty sure we all visualized it going down a bit different than it did. He told us to wait at the bottom of the stairs and his guy would come pick us up. I remember our conversation while we were waiting and all of it had to do with where Frank keeps his fishing boat. We had scoured the island quite a bit and didn't remember seeing one so we figured maybe he called a friend of his to take us or it was hidden away in the interior of the island on one of the rivers. We were wrong on both accounts!

Slowly coming around the corner we see a glorified canoe with a motor on it. On the back sitting Indian style was, Jose, one of Frank's staff. As we were waiting for the boat to stop, I thought to myself, surely we weren't going fishing on the Pacific Ocean in this. After a brief moment of anxiety while boarding, I sat down very cautiously and thought to myself again, God didn't bring us this far to throw us in the ocean and be eaten by sharks so let's roll with this and see how it goes. Well I can tell you this, we felt like a gnat on an elephant's butt. It seemed like the ocean would just swallow us at any moment but after a short period of time it was clear Jose knew what he was doing and as they say, "This wasn't his first rodeo". There were definitely some anxious moments when a fifteen swell was headed towards us or when we spotted a huge volcanic rock formation piercing through the water that we felt surely was unavoidable but after a while it was more relaxing than riding on a cruise ship. So we fished for a few hours until twilight and hauled in a few yellow tails that would end up on our dinner plates in the very near future. These are the types of experiences that shape our perspective on the world and they are so different every place you visit. As Sydney J. Harris puts it, "Regret for things we did can be tempered by time; it is the regret for things we did not do that is inconsolable".

After another night of jungle music and deep thoughts, we were headed home. Often on your way back from a trip of this magnitude your mind races. What could we have done different? What happened at home while I was gone? How long will it take for me to catch up? Will I take what I learned on this trip and apply it to my life? Can I inspire others to do more? Where will God's Path take us next? Well as I pulled in my driveway and went to the mailbox, inside I found check for almost the exact amount that we went over budget because of the unexpected flight we had to take. For me, as I stood in my driveway staring at this check in disbelief, with a tear in my eye, all I could think about was how I should have never doubted for a second that God would not provide. He has shown us grace at every turn and no circumstance we face will ever change that.

On our most recent trip to Panama it truly felt like we had never left. Every time I return to Bongo, I get a since of peace. My mind slows down and a greater appreciation for all the things we take for granted on a daily basis are thrown right in my face. It is a very intimate experience for the guys that go. It gets dark early because of how close it is to the equator, so when you are done for the day, we have a lot of time to reflect on our experiences that day and invest in one another. When you are in the jungle, there is no rat race, no cell phone, just life!

Our goal for this trip was to establish a presence in Sortova that would be sustainable for years to come. All of the baseball equipment and Turface products we donated on previous trips had been moved to this community. After visiting the first day, there was renewed hope for what could be done but it required building relationships with the local representative, school principal and the physical education teacher. This started with a game of softball on Sunday afternoon that included the adult males from the community. Next it was P.E. at the school and that progressed to baseball clinics by the end of the week. We gave the kids hats, socks, shirts and donated equipment to the school so that training could continue after our departure. One evening we went to Concepcion to speak with a local soccer club about our experiences and how sports can be such a driving force in effort to serve others regardless of their circumstances. We also took two afternoons to redo the ceiling of a local church in Bongo called, Iglesia Evangelica Metodista. Of course a trip to Bongo would not be complete without a few relaxing trips to the river. By the end of the trip we were invited to a dinner hosted by the local representative that the Governor even attended and we secured spots for interns the following summer.

I think sometimes not knowing what's coming is better especially when it comes to "Volcan Baru Part 2". I tackled this beast when I was four years younger and it was the hardest thing I had ever done physically then. So to say I was a little apprehensive would be an understatement. As a leader however, that can't show on your face or in your body language. On top of that I had the great idea for us to spend the night on top so we had twice as much gear and supplies. Wouldn't you know by the time we reached the final 2 kilometers, it was raining sideways and freezing cold! So what do you do, give up or push on, of course you push on just like life! By the time everyone reached the top we knew or plans for pitching tents and starting a fire were out the window. There would be no singing "cum bah yah" around the camp fire. Fortunately for us, there is a police station on top of the mountain so we ended up sleeping on the floor in a storage room. Wet, cold and huddled together our goal was just to make it through the night by tending to the guys that were suffering from altitude sickness and figuring out how to use the bathroom without indoor plumbing during a freezing cold rain storm and 40-mile per hour winds. It was interesting to say the least and no doubt for everyone an unforgettable experience.

We finished this trip on the Pacific Ocean. Of course, in typical fashion we headed towards a destination unknown but with some sort of general knowledge about the area. We did know if we kept driving, we would eventually hit the ocean. When we finally pulled in to this little gravel parking lot and open the van doors, you could hear the unmistakable sounds of waves crashing against the sand. There was a little outdoor restaurant with a covered tin roof and plastic tables and chairs. As we all walked through the sand of this deserted beach, we turned around and there was Volcan Baru as the back drop. It is hard to explain the range of emotions you feel. You have the euphoria of eight foot Pacific Coast waves and the beautiful Costa Rican mountains off in the distance but yet that replay over and over in your mind of a brutally exhausting climb to the top of that mountain. It was actually a perfect combination of all you are and all you strive to be. Of course after pulling some tables together and sitting down to relax, a storm sweeps in off the coast and we were right in the middle of a lightning storm. It was like being at a 4th of July fireworks show. Being from the south, I am not usually too keen on storms because a lot times that means tornadoes but for some reason it was very tranquil. As I looked around at the guys hanging out with each other, thinking about the entire week coupled with all these breathtaking features, all I could think to myself was, this is perfect!

CHAPTER 6
AFRICA

On be-known to us, our work in Panama had not just helped change the culture of a small farming village but evidently was being noticed half way around the world. The Youth Council of Limbe, Cameroon saw pictures and read our story on Facebook. That's all the evidence I needed to show me that "social media" has truly changed the way we live. So over the course of several months, I communicated via email and planned our next trip to introduce the game of baseball to over 300 kids that had never seen a bat, ball or a glove before. During this time, I did the best I could to come up with a comprehensive itinerary with limited communication and a lot of faith. When I introduced the idea to our community, to say they were a little apprehensive would be an under-statement.

There weren't too many mommies lining up to send their sons half way around the world to a continent that had just experienced an "eboli" outbreak and was only a few countries away from where we were going. I even had to show my daughters how far apart the two countries were to reassure them there was no danger. Now just because there was no danger from a deadly disease, doesn't mean it was the safest place in the world either. In the hour and a half, it took from the airport in Douala to Limbe we took a short cut to avoid bandits and were stopped twice by machine gun carrying guards. They were supposed to be check points but all it was, was a shake down!

They asked for all of our passports and that's when our driver, Dominque, went to arguing with these people. He knew what they wanted and he wasn't having any of it. It was a very tense scene watching someone we just met fight so passionately for us and I would like to mention again these guys were armed. All we could hear him say while his arms were moving and pointing in the air was that these men are here to help our children and no one should be trying to take anything from them. We often discussed what we thought might have happened had he not been with us. At no point during our trip was he going to allow anyone to take advantage of us. Dominique was a God send from the beginning until he dropped us off at the airport.

Now unfortunately not everyone was as honorable and it took us almost two days to figure out who was really there in an effort to further our cause and who was there trying to execute their own agenda. The later was definitely more common. When you live in the United States we are so naive about the desperation people face on a daily basis and the hopelessness they feel. Come to find out, people were trying to use our organization and the work we were doing to elevate their status in the community in hopes of acquiring visas for their families.

At the end of the day, none of these obstacles changed our mission, it just made it a little more difficult. We started by doing an interview at the local Christian radio station in hopes of creating interest for a sport that had never been played before. Would kids and their parents even show up? Yes, I had been told by leaders in the community they would come but you truly never know until you show up and in this case even after you show up. Our first location was beside a corn field on the out skirts of town in close proximity to what they would consider a neighborhood. We showed up and there were three kids kicking a soccer ball.

My heart dropped! "Well boys, we didn't come here to sit in the van." We got out and starting throwing the baseball around and I kid you not, in 20 minutes there were over a 100 kids in that field. They were coming from everywhere it seemed like. It felt like I was in that seen from *Field of Dreams* when players from the past started coming out of the cornfield to play ball. The most famous line of that movie, "Build it and they will come", kept replaying over and over in my head as this was happening. After my amazement wore off, we had to figure what to do with over 100 kids that had never swung a bat or thrown a ball. The kids put gloves on both hands, used the wrong end of the bat and certainly had no idea how throw a ball.

My main concern was safety and the kids having a good time. Luckily for us we had a lot of whiffle balls. Our photographer had a drone so that was a huge source of entertainment watching kid's chase it around in total amazement. They were just as amazed to see their picture on a camera as was evident by the swarms of children surrounding the cameraman when he allowed even a glimpse into what he was taking pictures of. Despite not knowing anything about the sport of baseball, the kids had a blast and several of them picked it up very quickly. It never ceases to amaze me regardless of what country, demographics or economic circumstances; kids are just kids! They all have smiles on their faces and completely appreciate any amount of time you are willing to share with them.

This pattern continued for several days in multiple locations throughout the community. In some places the kids were older, the facilities may have been a little different but in each place one constant remained, a desire to experience something new despite what circumstances they maybe be facing as soon as they left those fields. Some of the young men we worked with were so gifted athletically and were so easy to work with. If they lived in the United States, they would be preparing to play major college athletics, instead they would leave those fields and prepare the next day for the fishing boat or the coffee fields. It's an eye-opening experience for someone on these trips to finally realize just how fortunate they are to have every opportunity in the world to succeed. Until they see this first hand, they have no idea that in places all over the globe, that's just not the case.

When developing any itinerary for these trips, of course you have to be prepared for the fact that some things just are not going to work out. For this trip, my contact told me there were American soldiers working with the Cameroonians at their naval base in Limbe. So of course I thought it would be a great idea to visit them and let them know how much we appreciate their service and even invite them to join us when working with the kids. So as we approached the main gate with anticipation at our scheduled time and were met by soldiers carrying automatic weapons claiming they had no idea what we were talking about, it didn't shock me in the least.

Dominique proceeded to haggle with one of the guards, which was definitely a common occurrence when we tried to do anything for anyone or with anyone on a daily basis. After they spoke we were told to wait off to the side in a small field while this soldier asked around. After about 20 minutes, a gold armor platted Toyota Hilux, drove through the gate and approached us. The two guys in the truck just sat their sizing us up, so not knowing what to do, I got out and went to talk to them. You could tell as I started speaking, they were on edge, checking their 360 constantly. So I started telling them our story, what we were doing in Cameroon and we just wanted to spend time with them if possible. The guy in the driver's seat, I later found out was the Commanding Officer (Chili is what they called him), looked at me and said, "No one knows we are here."

After he said that, I knew these guys were an elite group here for a specific reason, so the edginess made sense. The more we talked however, you could tell he felt more at ease and they actually invited us back to their hooch. After introducing us to his team, we just sat down and hung out. We told them about our plans for the week, asked them if they would like to be a part of it but anytime we asked a question about anything relating to their group, every soldier immediately looked at Chili as to say, can we answer that? It was a unique experience to see that dynamic unfold in front of us. These guys were the best of the best and you could tell it. They were all ripped, muscles everywhere and the humblest guys on the planet. It truly made me proud to be in the same room with them and come to find out a few of them played college baseball.

So during the week they came and helped with clinics, we took them out to dinner one night and we even played beach volleyball with them. I felt like we were in the movie, Top Gun. At the end of the trip, the night before we left, we went back to the base and gave them baseball equipment so they could even play with the Cameroonian soldiers they were training. They presented us with patches, decals and not only that, proceeded to tell us how much of an amazing week it was and how much they appreciated being a part of it. I can remember listening to these words and thinking to myself, I can't even reveal these guys names because their families don't even know where they are and he is thanking us. This was not the highlights you see on CNN; we were standing in the midst of sacrifice these guys make on a daily basis for our freedom. It was such a privilege and an honor to be around them for just the briefest of moments but it also confirmed for me how the smallest act of service to others can impact lives in the most unlikely of places. I will never forget the time we spent with those young men and I am quite sure they will never know the life lasting impression they left on me.

Another very eye opening experience for us was visiting the Slave Trade Port of Bimbia. This was one of the major slave ports on the West African coast for over 200 years. According to locals, not much has been documented here until recently because it has remained hidden under thick tropical rainforest but mainly because villagers of Bimbia believe the area is cursed; as they explained it to us, "no one who ever went there ever came back!" Regardless of how uncomfortable it was, I felt it was extremely important for our team to learn about this awful time in history and invest our hearts and minds in this beautiful country.

I am not going lie, it was kind of eerie walking this long path lined with huge bamboo pods, lush green trees, flowers and the sound of waves crashing in the foreground knowing what I thought may lie ahead. As we drew closer to our destination, the hairs began to stand up on the back of my neck and all I can say is I felt a strong presence as we began to look upon these ruins that were being taken back by the jungle. I couldn't take my eyes off of these stone troughs that slaves would have to eat out of while being chained and shackled. Believe it or not, that wasn't the hardest pill for me to swallow, it was the "door of no return"! There was a small river that ran up into the jungle from the ocean and built on its bank, was the last place these slaves would ever see of their homeland. Basically it only consisted of stone pillars equipped with the chains of bondage and two doors; one to come in and the other facing the river where these young men and women would walk through and never be seen again.

Recent historical findings have documented nearly 200 slave ship voyages that left Cameroon bound mostly for plantations in the Americas. These ships would anchor on Nicholls Island just off the coast and send small boats up the river. As we were listening to this very vivid depiction of events, you could see mouths drop, eyes get big and even streams of tears. It is really hard to explain the emotions you go through, if you have never been to such a historically significant and at the same time an unbelievably horrific place. It is quite certain one of, if not the most powerful place I have ever been.

CHAPTER 7
COLOMBIA

One of trips was to the interior of Colombia. Contrary to popular belief, baseball is not given much thought there on a daily basis. When talking to people back in the states about the upcoming trip, they assumed all Latin American countries love baseball but the truth is, soccer is still king! Our team for this trip was by far the biggest group to date, 26 servants, ranging from ages 16-52. Our team represented several local high schools, colleges and leaders from the community. I truly believe it's a testament to not only our prior work to date but God's Path for "More Than A Game" and all of its volunteers.

One of our goals for this trip was to introduce baseball to children in Puente Iglesias, a small village at the base of the Andes Mountains. We would also give them baseball equipment, uniforms, bibles and hopefully some sort of structure to continue training after our departure. We would spend 5 days in the country at a beautiful farm house, locally known as a "Finca", so graciously provided by Patrick Powers. It was located about half way up one of the mountain passes over-looking the river. The views were breathtaking and really left you in awe as we watched the sun come up or clouds roll in below us. I don't think any of us had ever stayed above the clouds before. The boys would get up at 6:00

am every morning and pick fresh fruit and get eggs from the hen houses. We also had a list of chores for them to complete around the farm during our time there. Patrick is a businessman from Texas, originally from Chicago that spends a good deal of time in Colombia. He felt our organization could not only help the kids of this region learn about baseball but also open doors for them that could change the course of their lives forever.

Six months prior he helped obtain Visa's for two young men, Jose Mercado and Mateo Porras in hopes of them returning with us to pursue their dreams of getting an American education and playing baseball in college. After just a few days with these two wonderful young men, several guys had already offered to open their homes to Jose and Mateo upon our return to the states. Before we started clinics on a Monday, we took a horseback ride through the mountains to the city of Jericho at about 9,000 ft. above sea level. Not many of us had much experience on horses and there were a few tense moments when the trails narrowed and you could see rocky gorges several thousand feet below. All that seemed to fade away as we came around this one turn and the all inspiring Andes Mountains were in full view for everyone to see. It's really hard to describe the beauty. To me, it feels like you are looking at a painting even though you know it's real, it still looks fake. We stopped for lunch near the top that consisted of rice, pork and plantains wrapped in a banana leaf. While we were eating, one of the horses got spooked and started a chain reaction that pulled most of the rickety barbed wire fence out of the ground and scared us all half to death.

After lunch we made our way to the top of the mountain and took a short break at the top to visit with a farmer and see the process of harvesting coffee beans. During this stop he invited us to have fresh bananas with him and just hang out for a while. If you have never had fruit freshly picked, I highly recommend it. It will blow your mind how much different it tastes than buying it from a store in the states. It hasn't been processed, preserved and shipped yet, so not only is it sweeter, it even smells and looks different. I had experienced this before in Africa when getting a pineapple on the side of the road, also picking oranges off the trees in Panama and even the first morning in Colombia when we had freshly picked mangos with breakfast. We tend to think everything is better in America but that goes back to getting out of your comfort zone and experiencing new cultures. There are so many things in this world we are completely ignorant about. We just accept what we know to be true because that's the path of least resistance!

Shortly after this we all loaded up on a really cool bus that took us to Jericho. This bus had open sides, wooden bench seating and was painted every color of the rainbow. They dropped us off in the town square at one of the most beautiful churches I had ever seen. After walking through the church we split up into groups, nosed around in several small stores and checked out the open air market on the plaza.

The next day we climbed a volcano, Sierro Bravo (10,800 ft.). One noticeable difference from the volcano in Panama was being covered by the jungle canopy for just about the entire hike. This made the humidity much worse. This hike was also straight up the face so you definitely had to do more climbing. That being said, there wasn't the long stretches of vertical walking like in Panama so it took us only about 3.5 hours. When one of my dear friends of over 20 years, Mike Getkin, made it to the top, he dropped like a sack of potatoes and curled up in the fetal position. Not bad for someone in his mid-fifties though! When he finally got up, all I could do is hug him and tell him how proud I was of him. I will never forget sharing that experience with him. We had lunch, took pictures, got some video footage and soaked in the moment before heading back down.

When I took a moment to look around, I could genuinely see the sense of accomplishment on everyone's faces. It is always amazing to watch the guys interact with each other while pushing themselves physically and mentally. You can learn so much about people when they are put in extreme circumstances. Are you going to give up in life when it gets hard or are you going to push through it and become a better person for having persevered during the tough times? That's really what it's all about and they all passed with flying colors. Believe me when I tell you, that hike was no joke!

The next morning, we headed to the village of Puente Iglesias to do a baseball clinic for all the kids in the school there. Because of construction on the bridge, we had to carry all the equipment we planned on donating about ¾ of a mile to the field. When we finally arrived at the field we were going to use, there was a man there weed eating grass that was waist high. As I told you earlier, not many things go according to plan on these trips. Expect the unexpected and just roll with it. We split into to four large groups and taught the kids throwing, fielding, hitting and base running. There were even three of the local Policia that stopped by and participated. After we were finished we presented the principal of the school with 10 bags of equipment, dental supplies and 100 bibles.

The second half of our trip would take place around the city of Medellin. With almost 3 million people, different challenges would lay ahead with the biggest being transportation. Despite this, we arranged to do clinics and equipment donations in Envigado and Santa Margarita. We also met with the Mayor's sports organization, Inder, in hopes of promoting baseball in the city. In the end, it was about the kids we spent time with and how they blessed us every day.

One day at a clinic in Envigado, several of the moms went home and made empanadas for everyone just to show their appreciation. In Santa Margarita, one of the kids went to his house during the clinic to get us water to show his appreciation. It's hard to explain the feeling you have inside when something like that happens because you can see all around you the circumstances in which the kids live (no running water, etc.) and their first thought is to provide for you. It is extremely humbling to say the least!

After doing clinics during the day, it had been arranged for us to play the Medellin Select Team in a three game series at the Stadio Medellin Villeges. We didn't put the roster for this trip together to play real games but we made the most of it and the kids had a blast. We made flyers and had the boys pass them out during the day to promote the events. When the lights came on, the little kids showed up! Our kids were signing autographs before the games just like they were in the Big Leagues! They never stopped smiling from start to finish. One of the local kids passed his phone to the dugout and the message read, "You are our idols!" That had a big impact on the boys; how we take for granted something as simple as playing a baseball game.

With the help of Pat Powers and the willingness of the Envigado Cubs baseball team, we were able to go back two more times and really establish a presence in that area. On these trips we renovated their field and established English speaking applications on IPAD's we donated. It was really cool to see these kids buy into the fact that education was truly their weapon to battle poverty and that service to others could change the course of their future. Honestly, it felt like I was at Glenwood. The family atmosphere was so cool and seeing kids from several years ago still in the program, let me know that the leadership there had bought in and they were going to change a lot kids' lives. Oh and by the way, Jose and Mateo that started on this journey with us several years ago, just finished playing baseball at Concordia University in Chicago and I am happy to tell you that both have received Bachelor's degrees!

Selfishly, my family got to come with me on the last trip and experience this beautiful culture so it wasn't just daddy's stories anymore, they got to see it firsthand. While working there, we stayed in apartments only two blocks from the field so it definitely had a strong local vibe. We ate at local café's every morning and had street meat every night. We had some time while staying in the city to do some site seeing which included the Aquarium and Botanical Gardens. We even added a hiking adventure with locals to their favorite waterfall. Of course, it took about three more hours than expected and was a lot harder than we were lead to believe but that's why this trips are so special. If you are willing to just put yourself out there, let your guard down and enjoy whatever comes your way, trips like this can really change your entire perspective on life.

Pat was so gracious enough to let us finish the trip by staying at the "Finca". It wouldn't have been complete if everyone didn't get to see the intense beauty of this place. We hiked Sierro Bravo again, with one exception, it was in a rain storm. Such is life, when adversity hits, you just push through it. We were all muddy, soaked to the bone and a little bruised up (Brianna must have fallen twenty times) but we made it! We hung out around the fire, told stories about our time there and fellowshipped until the wee hours of the morning. Brianna even got to take her senior pictures. Sawyer got up at sunrise and took the most amazing pictures of her. I'm not going to lie, I was a little sad watching her pose and look all grown up for those pictures but at the same time, so proud of the young lady she had become. Beside the pictures being absolutely breathtaking, I was so proud to see how both my daughters had matured because of these trips. What a blessing for my wife and I to experience these adventures with them.

CHAPTER 8
DOMINICAN REPUBLIC

With the help of Pittsburgh Pirates' Latin American Pitching Coordinator, Amaury Telemaco, as well as support from the Pirates' Charities Foundation, the Pirates' Academy and Turface Athletics we achieved so much in such a short period of time. In just six days, we were able to build a field in La Romana, renovate a field in Boca Chica, administer two clinics, visit an orphanage, go to a Toro"s baseball game, go dune buggy riding, swim in a cave and visit the beach. We even managed to squeeze in Thanksgiving Dinner on foreign soil. We also introduced the first women of MTAG. Never before had we opened one our trips up to females and the fact that three of them were my wife and two daughters made it extremely special to me.

Our team consisted of 15 in all, ranging in ages from 12-60 and hailing from Alabama, California and Georgia. We had current high school players, former college and professional players as well as community leaders that had never played before. It was a great group with a lot to offer these two different communities. We had only decided a month before that we were going to make this trip happen, which is a much shorter time frame than normal. I had been introduced to Kyle Stark, Assistant GM of the Pirates, during the spring by a mutual friend, Anthony Randall. I met Anthony, a

Ranger and Chaplain for the U.S. Army, through a free-clinic we did that winter in Columbus, GA. We hit it off immediately and wanted to help us any way he could, which started with his contacts in the Pirates' Organization. After visiting with Kyle during Spring Training he agreed to help in any way possible. He started by making sure we had a significant donation of equipment for our trip to Colombia and put me in contact with their key personnel in the Dominican Republic and the Director of Pirates' Charities.

My first email was met with open arms and excitement for the prospect of us coming to the D.R. In preparing for this trip, I was already significantly impacted by developing a great friendship with Amaury. I knew right away after our first time on the phone we had the same passion for serving others as well as the same appreciation of all that God has blessed us with! So, it didn't shock me when he met us at the airport despite his busy schedule with the Pirates and that he made sure we were comfortable in our new surroundings before he left for the night.

Our team stayed at the Good Samaritan House, which consisted of dorm style accommodations, a common area for meals and a 30-year old school bus to take us anywhere we needed to go. An added bonus, the best dessert I have ever tasted each night after dinner from a little local bakery. No matter his schedule, our friend seemed to show for that part of the evening (we called it dessert with Amaury)! Our first day started outside the Toro's Stadium with a clinic and field building. When we arrived, the coach (Varon William) and his kids were waiting on us. Before we could start, he finished having church service with them. As we begin setting up to administer the clinic, it was a good opportunity to evaluate the piece of land available for a field. Basically, it was a forgotten piece of land tucked next to a water tower and beside a ten-foot high wall protecting it from the highway. Not to mention it was covered with boulders, trash and over burden. So what looked impossible to start became our mission for three days.

We immediately recognized that the only way that would happen, would be to rent heavy equipment and really get the coach and his players to buy into the project. Well that certainly happened and then some. We even made a backstop out of huge rocks and painted the "More Than A Game" logo on it. On Tuesday after we finished work for the day, we headed to the Ninos De Cristo orphanage to donate school supplies and children's books. The director was so appreciative and so were we for just having the opportunity to share time with those amazing kids. Before leaving La Romana's newest field Wednesday afternoon, we played games with the kids, donated equipment, uniforms, bibles and the coach and heavy equipment operators even got some cuts in.

That night we headed to a Toro's game to experience a Winter Ball game in the Dominican. It was non-stop excitement from start to finish regardless of what was happening on the field. There was a pep section with drums, chants and when they weren't cheering, which wasn't very often, loud music was blaring throughout the stadium. It was so much different from a game in the states, you could feel the passion they had for their team and the game of baseball. We saw a relief pitcher throw a pitch 100 mph and the mascot body slammed a stuffed dummy behind home plate! We had an amazing time.

We scheduled Thursday as a day of rest and planned an excursion for everyone. It started with dune buggy driving through coffee plantations, fresh water swimming in caves and finished with a visit to the beach. No one on the team had ever done any of those things before so it was a special day for all involved. That apprehensive look on people's faces before jumping into a cave is priceless and then when they hit the water and the temperature takes their breath away it's even better. Facing that uncertainty in any aspect of life is what builds character and confidence so that we can face challenges in life head on. We finished that night with a special Thanksgiving Dinner we had arranged away from the dorm.

After we returned, Amaury invited my family and me over to his house to hang out with him and his wife. We had a wonderful time just talking about what was going on in our lives, the trip up to that point and pretty much life in general. When people are genuine, most of time they want to talk about you and not themselves. You would have never known he played in the big leagues for 9 years because it was like sitting out behind my house watching college football with the guys on a Saturday afternoon. There were no hidden agendas just sincerity. Oh and his wife asked the girls if they wanted to take a hot shower and of course they couldn't get upstairs fast enough!

We headed out early the next day to Boca Chica to renovate a field near the Pirates' Academy. Unlike our first project, this field had a good framework and just needed a face lift. We started by edging and removing all the weeds from the entire infield. Then we built a mound, rebuilt the home plate area and added conditioner to the infield. The Pirates' Academy sent guys to do a clinic with the kids. They also helped us pass out all the equipment, uniforms, and informed us they planned on adding a fence to the outfield after our departure as well as committing field maintenance help on a monthly basis. We finished up by speaking with all the players and giving them bibles. That evening we headed to a spot Amaury recommended at a nearby beach to have dinner and have our MTAG Emmy Awards (a tradition we started in Colombia). Each person gets an award and gives a brief speech about their experience for the week and what the trip has meant to them personally. It is a great time of personal growth and fellowship.

Tim Fanning

The final morning, we were up early, out of the dorm and headed to the orphanage one last time. We wanted to donate some shoes and clothes before we headed out. Next we arranged to meet Coach William at the field in La Romana to give him Turface Moundmaster Blocks so he could build a pitching mound and home plate for the kids after we left. We also brought more equipment and clothing to be dispersed at a later date. He was so appreciative and prayed for us. It was a truly special moment! We had arranged to tour the Pirates Baseball Academy and have lunch before our flight left so that was our next stop. You could tell during the tour, that building servant leadership qualities in their players is a high priority. Quotes from Roberto Clemente, the name sake for the highest Community Service Award in the Major Leagues, adorned the walls. Operations Assistant, Emmanual Gomez, giving us the tour was very quick to talk about helping others in need and developing the man ahead of the player. It was quite impressive because I could tell it had been ingrained in him from the top of the organization. We had a great lunch in the cafeteria and probably would have eaten more but we were running short on time.

We arrived at the airport with just enough time to say our goodbyes. One group was headed to Atlanta and the other to San Fransico. It's hard to describe how close you can get to someone in just a week under these circumstances but I'm pretty sure it's because of the vulnerability you feel when taking on the unknown and pushing through whatever is thrown at you. It's very intense at times, allows us to let our guard down and really get to know one another. That includes our bus driver (Colbert) and our translators (Gia and Luis) as well. There were hugs, tears of joy and promises to stay in touch. One thing was for certain, none of us would ever forget these people or this experience.

Our next trip was different because we got to stay at the Pirates Academy with the players and coaches. Our goal for this trip was to completely renovate the field in El Mamoon. After taking several trips, you have an idea what that means but you never know until you are actually on sight. This particular field was completely over grown. I mean you couldn't even see the infield dirt so the first order of business was getting all the weeds out. After this, we ordered several truckloads of dirt to build it up and completely edged out a new diamond. Next, we built a new mound and then painted the backstop. We finished by digging drainage ditches around the entire field to keep those afternoon showers from ruining their day. This was a lot of back breaking work but we had a great group which included our newest member of the team, Amuary Telemaco Jr.

His father and I had been talking a while about him coming to the states to play baseball for his senior year. I felt this would be a great opportunity for him to get to know a lot of the guys and he stayed with us at the Pirates Academy. Every day after we finished working, we would have clinics to cap off the day. We did notice however, that every day there were more and more kids showing up. I guess the power of "word of mouth" advertising was alive and well in this neighborhood. Our plan was always to finish the week with a big clinic and donate all the equipment but as the numbers kept growing, it made me a little uneasy. After thinking about it one night, I decided we would give the coaches of the local teams that played at that field the equipment and let them pass it out. I have been in situations before when giving out equipment has turned a little dicey before. Some people in that environment would use this as an opportunity to profit off the items you are donating, a lesson we learned all too well in Africa. That's why I have learned to include the coaches because they know exactly who needs the equipment and who doesn't.

As much as you try to prepare for all scenarios, sometimes you just can't and besides, what's the fun it that. That being said, one of our volunteers decided to give away a few things before we were finished and that turned into a fire storm. Before I knew it, we were completely surrounded by hundreds of people and action had to be taken. I am responsible for the safety of everyone on the team and before it got out of hand, I loaded everyone on the bus and we hit the road. Now, were we in any immediate danger, maybe not but before it had a chance to escalate any further, we got out of dodge. It definitely gave the kids something to embellish about on our trip back to the Pirates Academy. I love listening to kids tell stories, no matter how farfetched they are because it means they are engaged and not being a knot on a log.

I mentioned Amaury Jr. (we just called him Junior) joining the team, well that didn't just mean the baseball team, that meant my family. Junior came to live with us and go to school at Glenwood. It was definitely an adjustment for us but for him as well. Now that I look back on it several years later, I definitely could have done some things different and I am sure he would tell you the same thing. For one thing, all I have raised is girls, so having another male in the house was an adjustment. I have tried my best over the years not to coach my daughters so I could just be a dad to them. Well, Junior played for me and lived with us, so it was difficult knowing where to draw the line in our relationship. I wanted him to be the best he could be, so I was pretty tough on him.

In retrospect, maybe I should have been a bit more understanding that it had to be extremely tough on him as well. Imagine moving to another country, where you don't know anyone while having the expectations on you of being the son of a former Major Leaguer. I definitely could have done a lot of things different but I wouldn't change that experience for anything in the world. He is such a great kid and just like my relationships with all my former players, I feel it has only gotten better as years have gone by. By the way, he signed with the Los Angeles Dodgers at the end of that Spring and still comes back to visit his friends in Alabama as often as he can.

The most recent trip to the Dominican was a bit different than in years past. Our goal was not to renovate or build fields but to start MTAG programs in four different cities: La Romana, San Pedro De Macoris, Bani and San Cristobal. This would be done by administering clinics and equipment. We would also have the privilege of visiting a local orphanage and painting a church (Iglesia Africana Methodista Espicopal) in one of their communities. We once again stayed at the Good Samaritan's House with seven girls and six boys. I point that out because we've never had more girls than guys on a trip before and I feel that means we are headed in the right direction. If girls feel comfortable going on trips with us than that tells me what we are doing is way more encompassing than baseball. They are obviously growing as people or they wouldn't continue to go.

One thing we've noticed over the years, no matter what country we are in and the amount of blood, sweat and tears we pour into a community; if we can't establish leadership and develop structure it will fade away very quickly. With the help of Amaury and Gavi Nivar (Pirates Academy Coach) we identified these cities as having desire to not only develop great baseball players but quality young men. Even in a country such as the Dominican Republic where major leaguers seem to grow on trees, the reality is that over 95% of these kids will never make it to the "show"! For several years now, I've seen these kids playing baseball on rocky, weed covered fields all day, every day. So if they don't make in baseball, then what? What do they have to look forward to for the rest of their lives?

Yes, we provided each one of these communities with equipment and uniforms but more importantly, a strong message. A message that baseball does not define them, there is more. It starts by becoming educated, accountable and above else; putting others ahead of themselves. What is so crucial for us, is who we put in charge when we leave. After meeting these coaches and spending the week with them, it's obvious they have a passion for serving others and helping these kids become the best versions of themselves. It has always been our goal to impact the country not just on the field but in the way kids see life in general. They can become leaders and a source of inspiration to others without hope.

CHAPTER 9
COSTA RICA

Well in typical MTAG fashion, we headed for a destination unknown. This time it was San Jose, Costa Rica. Through our relationship with Secundino Morales in Panama, connections to the Refuge of Life in La Carpio (a barrio outside of San Jose), took us to a tremendous place of need. We were told this was one of the worst areas in San Jose, that there was only one road in and out and only one piece of land that was not concrete in the entire barrio. Sounds just like our kind of place! The team spent the week not only teaching baseball but also working on a community center in the Las Grades neighborhood.

As mentioned in previous chapters on almost all of our trips, there seems to always be an element of surprise upon our arrival. This time was no different. The community center was an ongoing project and its director (Marielos) was one of the sweetest ladies I have ever met. You could tell she had poured her heart and soul into this place. When we walked these narrow, trash littered streets with her, I felt a Mother Teresa like aura and connection with almost every family we encountered. It would always take us longer than anticipated to get started each morning because of all the hugs and loving Spanish chit chat. Honestly, I felt like we were back in the states walking the streets with a celebrity stopping to sign autographs. However, that's not the surprise, this squatters' community (no official property titles), take what you can get, was only accessible by 120 steps!

Of course, the community center was at the very bottom by the river so everything used for construction had to be delivered by hand. In the mornings, we carried bags of concrete, sand and cinder blocks up and down those stairs and in the afternoons we administered baseball clinics between rain storms. To say those stairs whooped our butts would be the understatement of all understatements. To make matters worse, we had kids helping us that crushed our egos even more. Some of those bags had to weigh as much as the kids but they just kept pushing. I'm sure some of it was to impress us but the underlying motivation was no doubt, their love for Marielos and wanting to be a part of something greater than themselves.

As we were going up and down those stairs, you really got to see the inner workings of this community. The houses are literally built on top and beside each other so closely that they share walls. Most of them have no floors or running water and usually sleep eight to ten people in less than 350 sq. feet. To even have the smallest place to go and play with their friends, be taught how to read and write or attend a bible study can be a huge source of relief and comfort. We really felt like what we were doing to help this community could change lives.

Serve to Lead II

The Refuge of Life was located at the end of the barrio and the descriptions were accurate. One road, the only piece of land available to do clinics and it was right beside the trash dump. Big garbage trucks were running all day dropping off trash so the noise was ever present but it seemed like when we started playing with the kids, the noise just disappeared. We could however see off into the distance; skyscraper size piles of garbage being pushed over in to these massive ravines. It was just another example of things we take for granted back home; having the space and technology to discard our waste and never give it a second thought. As I looked out over this beautiful landscape, it did sadden me to see it happening and I wondered just how many places around the world were probably in the exact same situation.

No matter how gut wrenching some things may be, I have learned through the years that a can't fix everything. That's why it's so important for all of us to serve others in need so that collectively we (as in mankind) can make a difference. That's why I thought it was so cool that the team shared lunch with other service groups from the United States that were there preforming medical missions. It was great to ask them questions about what they were doing and hear their own stories of triumph and compassion. By the end of the week, they even found their way out to the field for some baseball with the kids as well.

On a personal note, we stayed at a really cool boutique hotel. We had great breakfast every morning and the hotel was only a block away from this little market (tienda) that was fully stocked with our favorite Latin American drinks and snacks. On our day off we got in that rental car and headed for the closest volcano we could find, Arenal (5,436'). It took us about 3 hours to get there but we were so excited. No we didn't hike it but instead, Payton Zeigler, arranged an extreme adventure course high up in the canopy for us that included zip lines, rope courses, repelling and even a Tarzan swing. The swing took you out over a 200-foot water fall and then you got to repel down it the. The last zip line was superman style and it was so fast and so much fun. Our guide even stopped to show us a pit viper on the trail that couldn't have more than a foot from us. We had lunch overlooking the volcano and finished the evening by stopping on the way back at a roadside cantina for dinner. Of course, it stormed the entire way and we got lost at least three times but no adventure is fully complete without a little adversity, right?

When our time had come to an end, we had spent an amazing week making improvements to the Community Center, established an on-going training program and donated enough equipment to keep this effort going forward for the foreseeable future. Our hopes were that we may experience the growth and longevity seen in Panama so we may again visit this beautiful country and continue to build our relationship with this amazing community.

CHAPTER 10
TAIWAN

Bryan Woodall has always been a big part of our organization but seeing as he was still playing professionally he had never been on a trip with us. He was always in season, so he could only volunteer with us during the Winter months which was always for local projects and clinics. When he signed to play for the Chinese Professional Baseball League in Taiwan, I definitely thought it would be several more years before he could travel with us internationally. Well after playing three years over there, we were talking in the off-season about the possibility of us bringing a group over to do clinics and donate equipment but to be honest, I never thought it would happen.

Of course, just like always, God has a better plan than I do. Bryan called me after Spring Training in 2018 and said he really thought we had a good shot at doing something great with his new team, the Fubon Guardians. He had met with their President, Joyce Chen and turns out that several people in their organization are Christians. He said they were very interested in partnering with us. Much like our goal in the Dominican of serving several communities, they wanted us to serve in multiple locations throughout the country. Logistically it would possible because Taiwan is a small island nation and everywhere they wanted us to go would be easily assessable by train. After seeing their plans, we were so excited for this opportunity and I personally was so grateful to Bryan for believing in us so strongly.

Usually, I am the one responsible for all the travel arrangements, equipment, clinic sites, volunteers, food, accommodations, transportation, site seeing, media, etc. Not this time! All I had to do was get us there. When we landed in Tapei City, we felt like rock stars. They rolled out the red carpet for us. We had our own bus, a tour guide and two translators with us the entire time. We brought $20,000 dollars, worth of equipment with us and we never touched it again until we reached whatever community we were helping that day. All of our hotels and meals were taken care of and they even arranged site seeing trips for us. I didn't have to do anything but immerse myself into a new culture, enjoy great food and teach the game of baseball. It was a once in a lifetime trip for sure.

When I tell you the itinerary was down to the minute, that is exactly what I mean. I remembering visiting Japan for the Winter Olympics in 1998 and their culture seemed to be the same way; very discipline, punctual, well dressed, strong work ethic, extremely business like and very clean. This was much different than all the other countries we had been to previously. As I mentioned in previous chapters, we could be scheduled to start at 9:00 a.m. and wouldn't start until noon. One of the first things I noticed, was even though we arrived to a city with millions of people, there was hardly a piece of trash anywhere. It was very modern and the architecture was beautiful.

After we got a good night's sleep at our hotel, Fubon had a big clinic planned at their baseball stadium the next morning. I am not sure what I expected, but holy cow did they do it up. We arrived to media (television and print) everywhere, interviews, speeches, dignitaries; you name it, they had thought of it. They had huge banners everywhere advertising the partnership. I know they were only being professional and doing it right but man it made me feel like a million bucks. After the festivities subsided, we had several hundred kids in attendance and it was back to doing what we love; teaching and giving! It was also really cool to see Bryan in his element. Everywhere we went with him, people would ask for his autograph. We saw tons of people wearing shirts with his face on them. I have known Bryan for a long time and he has definitely never been one to search out the spotlight but I was glad to see it had found him. He has always done things right and has always been selfless in doing it, so to see him in a place that truly appreciated him put a big smile on my face.

Anytime we go on trips, one of the biggest topics of discussion will always be cuisine. That's one of the coolest things about traveling abroad is experiencing local delicacies. I love getting people out of their comfort zone when it comes to eating and I would have to say that Taiwan definitely delivered in spades. We ate fish eggs, baby deer, fish skin and even tried "stinky" tofu. I am not kidding, that's what it is called and for good reason; it smelled so bad! A couple guys even tried 1000-year old eggs and that was hilarious watching them try to get those down. Even if we weren't that hungry, we would take a trip down to the night market and see what live specimens they were selling. It was, just like it always is, such a great educational experience to see another culture first hand and not just on television or in a magazine. Another thing we noticed very quickly is just about every restaurant was family style. They would bring out tons of items from the menu and everyone shared. Most of time, there was a Lazy Susan in the middle of the table, so when you got the amount you wanted, you put the serving dish back and gave it a turn until the next item was in front of you. Oh and there were definitely a lot of funny moments watching everyone try to use chopsticks.

Our tour guide's name was June, he lived in California for several years so his English was fantastic. His knowledge of the culture gave us a different perspective about the country for sure. We went to the National Museum, the Tropic of Cancer, Taipei 101 (the 8th largest building in the world) and even got to see some tribal ceremonies when we left the city and ventured out to the countryside. Our itinerary basically took us around the entire island. Each day we had a different community to work with and once we left the city, you noticed a drastic difference. There was a lot of farm land, lush vegetation and gorgeous mountain terrain. I am not sure what I was expecting but I wasn't expecting it to look like Hawaii. On one particular night we stayed on the ocean and it was probably the nicest hotel I have ever stayed at. Not because it was big and fancy but because it was nestled right at the base of a mountain and also over-looked the ocean. Man, the sunset was breathtaking. Of course, during one pit stop on the coast, our guys found their way down to the water and did a little cliff diving before we got back on the road.

One thing that I noticed no matter what community we were in, the kids were very discipline and extremely respectful. We never had to worry about kids getting out of line, they were there to learn and so were their coaches. All of the clinics went great, they were very appreciative of the equipment and the instruction. When the day was over, their coaches always had a parting gift for us. Daniel and Jean were our translators and they made sure nothing was lost in translation and even managed to get some cuts in when we played games with the kids. I remember how grateful I felt just being there, the backdrops were so beautiful, the people were so nice and then on top of that, doing what I love; doesn't get any better. I did think maybe King Kong was going to walk out from behind one those mountains at some point. That is just how untouched the landscape looked.

After the last clinic of the week, we were bused to a nearby school for an evening celebration. It turned out to be a covered dish supper provided by the kids' parents. They wanted to show us just how much they appreciated the time we spent with their children. That wasn't the best part though. Each school that had participated in the clinics from that area, prepared their own dance or chant for us. One by one, they came up in front of everyone and laid it down. Some of them had choreographed dances to American music, some were native dances and some were chants in our honor. It was one of the coolest experiences I have ever experienced abroad. We ate, fellowshipped and listened to music until it was pitch black dark!

Not that the trip didn't already exceed every expectation imaginable, the day before we were scheduled to depart, Fubon had arranged for us to attend their game and they rolled out the red carpet. Joyce made sure we had an executive suit, stocked with message chairs and boy that was nice! She even walked us around the stadium, got us souvenirs at the team shop and bought every one of us what we wanted to eat. She didn't have to do that, but that's how she was, first class all the way! To be honest, I wanted to stay another week but our time had come to an end and it was time to say our good byes and head west.

This is what Bryan had to say:

Having the chance to serve others alongside Tim has been an amazing and rewarding journey. Our respect and appreciation for each other runs deep, and I am grateful for the bond and friendship we have created over the years. I was so fortunate to help organize a trip to Taiwan for Tim and the group. I have always looked up to Tim, but this experience helped me gain an even deeper appreciation of his generosity and positivity towards helping others. The things that I have learned from Tim are invaluable, and I hope to continue to find more opportunities like this to build and grow for a very long time.

CHAPTER 11
PUERTO RICO

Our most recent trip to a new destination was a little different than most of our trips. We did have some field renovations planned but we also had several baseball games planned against different communities located in the southern part of the island. Over the years we have played a few games but it's not our usual cup of tea. Never the less, it would be a great opportunity to experience a different culture and try our best not to eat at any fast food restaurants. We don't run across that many on our travels but I guess that was to be expected since it's a U.S. territory. I tried my best to zoom on by them and all the teams we played against always had dinner planned so I only caved one time and took them to McDonalds.

We started off by renovating a local field. The plan was to de-weed the playing surface and paint all of the stands. Of course, it took us a while to get started because we had to watch BJ Snellgrove chase an Iguana for a half an hour. Evidently, in the 1970's they were brought to the island as pets and now they have become a full-blown pest control issue. The locals call them, "chicken of the trees". Well needless to say, he didn't catch it and we went to work. Unbeknownst to us, an old man that lived next to the field had been watching us and he showed up with a surprise. He had climbed up one of the nearby trees, caught one and brought it over for all of us to pet. The kids took pictures with it and we got back to work. Well about fifteen minutes goes by and he shows back up again with the iguana. There was one difference, it didn't have any skin on it. The girls were grossed out and the boys thought it was cool. Ok, back to work, we are never going to get this job finished. I look up about twenty minutes later and there the sweet old man stands again. This time he had a plate in his hand full of grilled meat and I am sure you know what it was. So in the matter of about an hour, we all went from wanting an iguana as a pet, to putting it in our belly. By the way, it did taste like chicken.

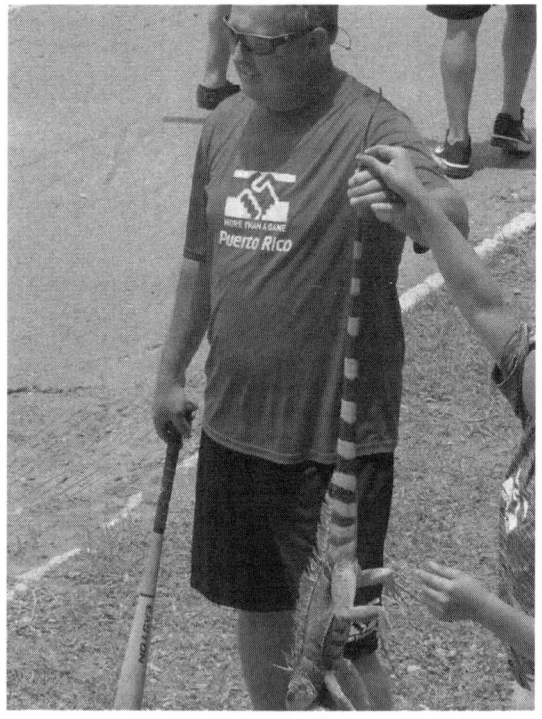

Let's just say the hunt became much fiercer as the week went on. One of our dad's on the trip, Jim Edwards, was chasing them with a baseball bat at one of our games. I felt bad at first but the locals assured us that it had to be done. They have no natural predator on the island, so they wreak havoc on the ecosystem. I guess it's no different than wild hogs in certain areas of the United States. Come to find out, it has become a staple in some lower income communities out of necessity. At the same field Jim was chasing iguanas, they dragged the field with a small car and a mattress before we played. I had never seen that before. Whatever it takes right?

Like I mentioned earlier, we would break bread with every team we played against after the game, so I figured that would be the best time to donate bibles and equipment. However, I wanted to do it a little different this time. I didn't want to give each team these things all at once, I wanted our kids to pick someone and go talk to them individually before giving them something. It was just another way to challenge them to get out of their comfort zone by having to communicate on their own. There is safety in numbers, so when you put them on an island like that, they have to dig a little deeper and figure it out. I didn't let anyone slide either, I made sure all of us did this at every location.

One night we were playing and the lights went out so it turned into a dance party. Our kids had a blast just dancing to local music, hanging out with the other team and their families in a social setting. That's one of the coolest things about Latin American culture, how close their families are. We never just hung out with the players, their families were always there cheering, cooking and loving the opportunity just to experience life with their children. Man, isn't that refreshing. No social expectations, no yelling at the coaches, no yelling at the umpires, no social media posts about how good their kids did; just pure joy! By the time the lights came back on, nobody even wanted to play anymore. The party even continued on the bus ride back to the hotel. Our transportation for the week was an old tricked out school bus complete with LED lights inside and out as well as big sub-woofers. We were bumping! It actually reminded me a lot of local transportation we saw in Panama City, several years earlier (one of them was called El Diablo).

We played in a really nice stadium the last day before we were scheduled to leave. There were two older gentlemen stationed in our dugout and they were two of the coolest dudes I have ever met. I guess they were there as ambassadors but never the less, they were so funny and so engaged with all of our kids. As I am talking to one of them, I find out he umpired in the Little League World Series in Williamsport. That's a big deal, so I started to ask him questions about it and upon further interrogation, found out something so cool. He was there in 1999 and that just happens to be when a team from our home town made it to the World Series. Seven of those players went to our school, get you some of that! I gave him an outfit from our trip and he gave me the sweetest jersey. It was a Puerto Rico, Hall of Fame jersey. It had pictures of Roberto Clemente, Ivan "Pudge" Rodriguez, Orlando Cepeda and Roberto Alomar on it.

We had great meals all week, but up until the last day, the one thing that had escaped us was the famous or should I say, infamous "pinchos". We saw stands everywhere during the week but our local contacts said we had to go to a specific place to get the best ones on the island. Well it was worth the wait, because they were outstanding. I had never seen that much barbecue chicken on one stick. You could barely hold it up with one hand. Little did I know, all this time that we were looking for "pinchos" and it was just their word for kabobs. Live and learn right but you better believe it tasted better just calling it a "pincho"!

As you've read about in previous chapters, all work and no play is not our M.O. We took the group to the beach one day and the kids decided to swim out about 300 yards to a small island for some exploring. When we all congregated at the snack shop before we were about to leave, Garrison McClary, thought it would be a good idea to jump off the deck over the water and try to wrangle a six-foot tarpon by hand. That didn't work out too well but I guess they are little bigger and faster than the fish we have in Alabama. This group didn't get to hike a volcano but there was a small mountain that we hiked. It was about 1000' but it was straight up, so for us old folks, it still got the blood pumping. That's another way of saying I was definitely out of breath. There was a Puerto Rican flag attached to a pole at the top. It was tattered and torn but flapping beautifully in the breeze. Everyone took their pictures next to it and we all picked our spots to chill and reflect for a little while. I remember thinking about that flag and how it is such a microcosm for all our lives. We are all tattered and torn in some way, shape or form but everyone is also beautiful in their own ways. Weathering those storms of life, gives us experiences to pull from in times of need and it tells the story of who we truly are.

Brianna had just graduated from high school a week before this trip. I told her she could go on a senior trip with her classmates but she wanted to go with us instead, so we decided to stay four extra days to celebrate her graduation. We went to Old San Juan which had fortresses and buildings dating back to the 1500's. If you have never been there before, the colors are so vibrant all throughout the city and there seems to be a café or an historical landmark on every street, so there was plenty to see. We also went to the island of Vieques. The first thing we noticed when we got off the ferry is that there seemed to be horses running around all over the island. Our cab driver told us that after the plantations there went out of business, they just let the horses go and now they run free. We even saw one on the side of road sleeping and I mean laying down on its side, like it was you or I sleeping in our own bed. Of course, at first glance I thought it was dead but the driver assured us that it was a common occurrence.

We spent all day at a secluded beach and finished that night by kayaking in a bio luminescent bay. Say that five times fast. I consider myself a world traveler but I had never heard of such a thing. I guess that's why you always ask locals where to go because it definitely ranks as one of the neatest things I have ever done or seen. Now, it took us a while by van to get there, it was pitch black dark and it smelled so bad (like sulfur) but once we got into that water and started moving, it's really hard for me to describe. The kayaks were see through and ever thing that moved in that water was like a fireworks display. Try to imagine being in a pitch black, dark lake and anything that moves is illuminated. This one is called Mosquito Bay and according to reports, it's the brightest in the world. There are only five known locations like this, world-wide.

These trips are so important not only for the service we may give but the deep seeded roots we return with. Each culture we experience is different in so many ways yet the one thing we always leave with is a greater appreciation and perspective on life. It is such a powerful force in determining how you choose to attack the rest of your life as a student, professional and even as a parent. "Nothing is more disgraceful than that an old man should have nothing to prove that he has lived long, except his years." Seneca

LEAD!

CHAPTER 12
SELF-PITY

"I never saw a wild thing feel sorry for itself. A bird will fall frozen dead from a bow, never having felt sorry for itself." Those words from D.H. Lawrence have always resonated with me. It is a very natural occurrence for people to feel sorry for themselves. We have all been there before. It is all too easy to blame someone else for our own shortcomings.

I wish I would have grown up with money, then things would be a lot different!

I wish my parents wouldn't have gotten divorced, then things would be a lot different!

If my coach would just give me a chance to play, then things would be a lot different!

I wish my boss could really see my potential, then things would be a lot different!

If he or she would just go out on a date with me, then things would be a lot different!

If my parents would have taken me to church as a kid, then things would be a lot different!

The list could go on and on, but I think you get the picture. We seem to live in a world of excuses instead of solutions! It amazes me on a daily basis the number of people I see walking with their heads down. If people would just look up and see the world that is right in front of them, there is no telling what they could accomplish. God puts so many wonderful opportunities in front of each and every one us, we just have to open our eyes. No one determines your fate and your ability to contribute to this world as a servant but you! It is essential that we all identify our strengths and weaknesses by being honest with ourselves. This allows us the ability to deal with failure in a more positive manner and not hide from it by feeling sorry for ourselves. "The essence of man is imperfection", Norman Cousins. An inability to do this can lead to depression; anger issues at home, a lack of focus professionally, obesity, alcoholism and even wavering in your spirituality. If we were all perfect, then what could anyone possibly have to offer us? How could anyone invest in us as people, if we have it all figured out already?

Self-pity affects kids, young adults, working professionals and the elderly. No one, regardless of age is immune to the self-pity disease. For example, most kids today are told all too often how good they are. Therefore, when they begin to fail at things and they will because everyone does at some point, they don't have the mental toughness to handle the situation. That's why it's extremely important for parents to prepare their children for when they aren't the "superstar". We are so afraid of our children's own failures; we can cripple them for life by shielding them from it. We should as parents point out positive contributions to the team and not strictly focus on the individual accomplishments. Eventually it will have to be a team effort for them to be successful regardless of what profession they chose as an adult.

Through years of experience I have noticed that the best player in youth sports is very rarely the best player in high school. Of course there are exceptions, but most of them have gone through puberty before most of their teammates and haven't really had to work very hard to be the best. As he or she gets older, many of those kids catch up physically and even pass the superstar because they had to develop work ethic to stay competitive. On top of that, it seems like this generation of parents live through their children and place such high expectations on them it ends up burning kids out. Unfortunately, instead of working to remain one of the best players, they give up on the sport all together and sometimes event resent their parents as a result. If we as parents are not able to accept our kid's mistakes, how will they possibly ever learn to cope with them? Hall of Fame coach, Rick Pitino, was quoted as saying, "Failure is good, it's fertilizer. Everything I've learned about coaching I've learned from making mistakes."

Young adults many times experience self-pity while in college or as they prepare to enter the professional world. Most often in college these problems surface in large part because of time management issues. Many are away from their parents for the first time and have so much free time they struggle because in high school almost every day is mapped out for them right up until time for bed. Therefore, young adults are not usually discipline enough to handle all of the extracurricular activities on top of a full class load until they figure out there is time for everything you want to do. So when they start doing poorly on tests, over sleeping for early classes and their love life is not going according to plan; you can bet late at night alone in their dorm rooms there are a lot of pity parties. Students that have jobs and/or play collegiate athletics have a little more success with time management because of a lack of free time but it is a struggle all the same.

When they get out of college or chose a profession without a degree this begins what everyone calls the "Real World". How many times have you said this to your kids, "wait until you get in the real world?" If you haven't yet, trust me you will. We all have visions and aspirations of the first job we are going to have and take the world by storm. As mature adults, we know for the most part that is not reality. Sometimes it takes people a life-time to find a dream job where they feel they truly are making difference and unfortunately it may never happen. So what do we do then, feel sorry for ourselves? I love what John Maxwell says in his book, Failing Forward, "The difference between average people and achieving people is their perception of and response to failure."

Self-pity is less prevalent in middle age professionals because most are in the midst of chasing a pot of gold at the end of rainbow (also known as the corporate ladder). Most are also busy taking their kids back and forth to athletic events, dance recitals or private lessons of some kind. It doesn't leave much time for self-pity, only sleep! However, this part of life is when many people begin to have regrets. I should have done this (sky diving, hang gliding, rock climbing, surfing, etc.) before I had kids, man I didn't know having a family would be this expensive and I can't travel as much because of our children's commitments. We have all said or thought this at some point in time, "I just wish I could do what I want to do for a change." With each passing birthday, these feelings are much harder to ignore. As Billy Crystal said in City Slickers, "Do you ever wake up and say to yourself; Is this the best I'm ever gonna look, the best I'm ever gonna to feel and it ain't that great?"

The truth of the matter is that we all share the same experiences in some way, shape or form. It's how we chose to deal with them as individuals that are sometimes completely different. We must not allow the negative thoughts to overcome the obvious blessings. Be inclusive when it comes to your family and truly invest in them and those pity parties will fade away. I am certainly not telling you to hurl your child out of an airplane or hang them off a rock face but go hiking with them, have them volunteer with you on community service projects, take them on trips when possible and just spend time with them that you will never have again. What this also does is build a family structure that will most times be repeated when your children become parents of their own.

As people enter their "Golden Years", they struggle with feeling relevant. They are on the backside of their careers and the younger version of themselves seems a distant memory. Everyone seems to know more about technology, drives faster than they do and has a much better solution to all the world's problems. In retirement especially, the days seem to last longer, become very irrelevant and certainly less fulfilling. It is essential as we grow older that we find a way to invest in others so that we find purpose in each and every day we are blessed with. No matter how much money we make, professional awards we accumulate or exotic places we visit, nothing we fill our cup and sustain us more when it matters most than serving others. We can all justify our feelings of self-pity no matter what walk of life we currently reside in but the only way to truly prevent it is by serving something greater than ourselves.

When I speak to groups, more often than not, self-pity is the main topic of discussion. I believe it's one of the biggest problems crippling our country today. We have enabled and spoiled our children to the point that makes it difficult for them to stand on their own two feet sometimes. We shield them from failure and everything always seems to be someone else's fault. Why does it have to be someone else's fault? Maybe things happen for a reason. Failure is how we learn to live!

Doctor visits have become the norm instead of for emergencies. As a teacher, I see it on a daily basis and as an Athletic Director I have begun to see it professionally with this generation. Kids miss more days of school and teachers seem to find it easier to call in sick. How can I preach to my players about pushing through adversity, if I am not willing to do the same? It ties directly in to that level of commitment we expect from them on a daily basis on the field and in the classroom. If we show kids they can perform when everything is not optimal circumstances, there is a good chance they will apply that to their professional life.

Up until I was diagnosed with cancer, I had missed two days in 20 years as a teacher. One was for an appendectomy and the other for the birth of one of my daughters. So do you think I haven't been sick during all that time? Therefore, at my house, "If I go to school, they go to school." In 15 years of school, starting in K-3, both of my daughters missed once. Do you think in all that time; they haven't been sick?

We used to call that "Tough Love" when I was growing up. Now when people use that term, this generation freaks out and parents are seen as abusive. It really has nothing to do with spanking children, all though I do not have a problem with that when necessary, but has everything to do with raising children that have a legitimate chance to impact the world in a positive manner. In my opinion, it's what we are sorely lacking in today's society. I have found my own definition of tough love and I call it "Raw Love"!

R – Respect: not only respect for parents, grandparents and teachers but for everyone you come in contact with regardless of like, dislikes, gender, race, creed or religion.

A – Accountability: be there when you are supposed to be and even when you don't have to be.

W – Work Ethic: it takes no talent to give effort and eventually you will be successful if you just refuse to give up.

L – Leadership: let them see you lead by serving others and put them in uncomfortable situations where they have to do the same.

O – Obedience: not only to parents, elders and bosses but to "God's Path" for their life.

V – Vulnerability: show them it's ok to let your guard down and truly pour your heart out, it's the only way to find true love, friendships and have a personal relationship with Jesus Christ.

E – Education: always strive to learn, not just in school, but about yourself, professionally and about your faith.

Raising children is probably the hardest thing in the world to do and at the same time the most rewarding. No one gets it right all the time and certainly not me but I do think if we all apply a little "Raw Love", the results will be noticeable and significant in the long run. I can promise you this, self-pity is not an option if we wish to leave this world better than we found it.

I found that out all too well during my battle with cancer. There were so many times that self-pity began to creep its way into my life. I was in pain. I couldn't travel. I didn't get to coach baseball. I couldn't eat what I wanted to eat. I am tired of changing these ostomy bags. I am tired of getting stuck by needles. I was trapped at home with nothing to do. I didn't know if I was going to live or die. First of all, what is the common denominator to all those sentences? Using the word "I" every time.

If you were to sit down and truly think about all the times you felt sorry for yourself, I bet a 100% of time, it never revolves around anything and anyone but you! That's why it's such a powerful source of depression and why the Devil will use it at the drop of a hat to get in your head. If we all constantly think of others ahead of ourselves, it flips the script. I can think of all those things I just listed but instead, this time think of all the ways those things negatively impact the people closest to me and it becomes motivation. They motivate me to get off my butt and fight! They motivate me to tell my story and appreciate everything in my life, including the trials and tribulations.

"Under no circumstance can you let Self-Pity win and expect to ever be the best version of yourself!"

CHAPTER 13
COACHING COACHES

My experience in leading on a daily basis just happens to be with coaches and student-athletes but you can apply these principles to any business model and be successful. This holds true if you are an: Owner, CEO, General Manager, District Manager, Supervisor, or Team Leader. While reading this chapter, insert these principles into your realm of expertise and I promise you will find small victories every day and be proud of the servant leader you become.

I was blessed to cut my teeth under two amazing men when I got into coaching almost 25 years ago. As I mentioned earlier in God's Path, Doug Key and Wayne Trawick took me under their wings when I first started coaching. You never felt like you were working for them, only that you were working with them. I think that is so essential as a leader because it will almost always maximize your potential as a coaching staff. If your coaches always just look at you as the "boss", they will truly never trust you and they certainly will not go the extra mile when necessary. You need to get to know them on a personal level. Get to know their families. Who are their favorite sports teams? What church do they attend? Do they like to travel? All these things matter! You want them to feel comfortable talking to you about issues that have nothing to do with your day-to-day business but everything to do with them as a person.

Look, we generally work 60 to 70 hours a week and we ask them to do the same. That sacrifice demands respect. We all know how much time we spend away from our kids, so be inclusive when possible. Invite their families and insist they be part of the process. I promise, if the significant other doesn't buy in, eventually the wheels will fall off! Athletic Directors or anyone in a position of leadership should want every program or department to be successful in its own right. Now does that mean every program is going to win a State Championship or every department will be the highest producing? No! What it does mean is every athlete you have that choses to "serve" your school should have every opportunity to grow in that sport and more importantly as a person. The same is true in the business world. If every employee you have doesn't serve the company and see the bigger picture, something is going to get missed and ultimately create deficiencies. They should not only be working for a paycheck but the ability to grow as an individual within a team environment.

Each one of us have an opportunity to help our coaches be an architect in building a program, from head coaches to assistant coaches. If we want our players to have criteria for making the right decisions, our coaches shouldn't be any different. How do your decisions effect:

1. Your relationship with God

2. Your education

3. Your family

4. Your sport

Make sure your vision for your Program is clear, concise and decisions should be made accordingly. It can't just be about winning! This does not work if the Coaches do not enforce the rules. It's the same for the best player to the worst player! Your players should know that they can't get away with something just because they go to an assistant coach instead of a head coach. In addition, if the rules are good enough for the players, they should be the same for the coaches! (I have left a coach at the hotel on the road before because he was late)!

Give your coaches, department heads, managers and employees their responsibilities in writing and hold them accountable. If you see areas that are not being taken care of, address it immediately. The last thing you need is for a prospective parent and/or student-athlete to tour your facilities and they see no pride in daily upkeep. What if your biggest vendor shows up for a surprise visit? Does that change their opinion of your company when they make decisions on who to purchase from? I often tell our guys that no one should ever walk past a piece of trash on campus and not pick it up. If you are too good to pick up trash, then you are too good to be a part of this program. The expectations have to be the same from top to bottom regardless of titles or salaries! (I have purposely put a piece of trash on the ground to see how many people will walk by it before someone picks it up)!

Sit down with your coaches each year and find out what they want and come up with a plan to get it. It needs to be face to face, not by email. The same can be said about texting. Never text important things to your employees. You can't feel intent or passion through an email or text! Obviously some schools or companies have more money than others, some may only have sweat equity to use but whatever the case, be involved and put the ball in their court. Make them share a vision with you for their teams and then use your experience and network to help. It may be something as simple as adding a new coffee bar to the break room. Doesn't cost much, but it goes a long way in showing your staff a little appreciation.

Coaches should do whatever it takes to show the community and their athletes that it's about more than them. Ask your coaches for suggestions when it comes to community service. Maybe there are groups or agencies they are familiar with that you have never worked with before. Maybe there is an opportunity that would be very important to them and not just to you. It is so vital as a company to give back to your community. How could you possible expect support or quite frankly even deserve it, if you are not willing to help your customers/patrons in times of need?

Make sure they know it is extremely important that you are always truthful with college coaches when recommending a player because you are building a reputation that will last forever. Every year the relationships you develop with coaches will continually grow and increase the pool that you can call upon. Because of your honesty in the past, they trust you and will give your players a legitimate evaluation. This will give your coaches tons of creditability in your community. Give them assignments to research certain schools you are targeting for players, always introduce them to college coaches at practice or conventions and ask them about their network.

There is no difference when it comes to business. I am firm believer that honesty always wins out. I know it's a tough pill to swallow sometimes when mistakes are made but right is right and wrong is wrong no matter how you try to slice it! Sure you can pull the wool over some people's eyes for a while but when the rubber meets the road, the cream while always rise to the top. Successful, long lasting, generational companies that have great reputations can be a positive impact on communities all over the world. Everyone wants to win or be successful, so what are you willing to do? More importantly, how are you willing to do it?

We need to really encourage our coaches and employees to attend State and/or National Conventions, Clinics, Trade Shows and Leadership Conferences. We should all want to get better as coaches/employees and this is a perfect way to do it. It also lets our players, parents, customers and vendors know we are serious about making our programs/departments better. It also gives us an opportunity to network with college coaches or business leaders and develop those relationships. If they are not interested in learning, there is a pretty good chance he/she will not be there long. Conventions and conferences can also be a great source for team building and a perfect opportunity for you to get to know your employees outside the workplace.

I think it's important to work with your coaches on their schedules. Each school is different when it comes to this. Some of you may have to make every schedule but if this is the case, at least give each Head Coach an opportunity to weigh in on what he/she wants. Talk to them about what they want to achieve through their schedule. It's not just a schedule as many people think, it can give them creditability within the community or just as easily hurt their reputation. Eventually, you may have them make the schedule and bring it to you to discuss before it's finalized.

I think it's extremely important to host Summer Camps. This gives your coaches another opportunity to reach the community and sell your programs. Put them in charge of scheduling, group assignments, registration, lunch and even passing out t-shirts. Make sure they know how to do it all and stress how important it is that players have another opportunity to volunteer and be role models for young kids that may end up playing in your program.

You may want to incorporate tours at your place of business and get local schools involved. Let them see what you do, promote your product and encourage them to be a part of it in the future. One of your future leaders could be in the audience. You will also find that your best employees will have no problem showing people around because they are extremely proud of what they do. Usually people who volunteer the quickest are the ones you can count on the most.

Meet with your coaches! Not only when there is a parent complaint, major scheduling issue, facility upgrade, or ordering uniforms but just to talk. These meetings can be very short, not even planned but very effective. Ask them how everything is going, if they need anything or just how their family is doing. They have to know, you do care about their success and not just when there is a problem! Make yourself available when possible to be in parent meetings with them. It will help keep the tension at a low and they will learn how to affectively speak with parents. Even invite them occasionally to sit in on a meeting with you. It can be with potential donors, sporting good salesmen, alumni, construction crews, etc. No different in business when you have a big client in town or a manufacturer you are trying to negotiate with. Being as inclusive as possible creates more ownership!

Your coaches or employees are extremely important to the long-term success of your program or business! They have to feel a part of the process if you want to maximize effort and effectiveness. It's our job as leaders to prepare them to best of our abilities to one day take our job. If not that, then take over another program or run another company. We should always want our best employees to want to be in the position we are in. If they don't, their potential is limited. This takes a little less ego and a lot more trust! I know sometimes it's hard to relinquish control but I promise it will pay off in the long run.

I love it when former coaches or players call to ask questions, it means they see me as a teacher and mentor. I'm not just talking about whether your former players and coaches are coaching in professional, college or high school baseball but what do they do with the knowledge they gained from your program. They may be coaching other sports, gone into administration or they may not even be in education at all. That is irrelevant.

When you see a special on TV or read an article about a famous coach's coaching tree or a very successful businessman's protégé going on to great success, many people don't actually understand what goes in to making that happen. It takes a lot of time, effort and commitment. I actually look at my coaching tree a little different than you might expect. My coaching tree has doctors, lawyers, salesmen, plumbers, electricians, helicopter pilots, realtors, managers, pharmacists and yes some professional, college and high school coaches in it. Eight of my former players have coached right beside me in our program. Several have moved on and been very successful at other high schools, colleges and even professional teams but my goal is not to produce great coaches, it's to produce great people!

When you see or talk to your former players and coaches, what do they want to talk about? What questions do they ask you? Are they still serving others regardless of their profession? How are they raising their children? Are they setting goals and pursuing them? If they are a coach, how do their teams play? What do their facilities look like? Are your former employees having great success at other companies or even in other industries? I bet their success or lack thereof is directly correlated to what they learned or didn't learn while they were under your leadership. Your philosophy is ingrained in them, so I would ask.

"What does your tree look like?"

CHAPTER 14
MAGICAL SEASONS

I can remember my first meeting with the team like it was yesterday; some things you just don't forget. As I approach almost 25 years in this profession and I begin to think back about truly special moments, some would be surprised when those memories are not from holding up State Championship trophies. Make no mistake about it, I am extremely proud of those on-field accomplishments because of how hard all the guys worked to achieve their goals and how unselfish each and every one of them had to be in serving something greater than themselves. It's the off the field memories that seem to spur more feelings of joy and accomplishment. I know eventually those victories will fade away but it's the hundreds of great young men lives I've been privileged to be a part of that matter the most. Helping them mature from adolescence to become better fathers, husbands and servants in this world. No one can convince me otherwise that our success over the years has been a direct correlation to putting all these other criteria ahead of winning.

However, I would be re-missed not sharing several truly special moments from years gone by. Some highlights and even low lights that somewhat paint a small picture of our program during my tenure. When you take over a program steeped in tradition as Glenwood, there are inherited expectations. They had not won a baseball state championship since 1993, the year Tim Hudson (4-time all-star, World Series Champion, Atlanta Braves Hall of Famer) graduated. Prior to that, the baseball program had won 14 state championships in 23 years of existence. So it would seem like the pressure was on me to win a championship but I never felt that way. I did have plenty of alumni tell me periodically, "You know we haven't won a championship in long time!" I was fine with it because I had confidence in what we were doing and how we were doing it. As you get older you gain such a greater appreciation of the process and not the results. The journey is so much more important and it's never more evident than when you take some time to really reflect on how you got there.

When you have coached as long as I have, the "grind" makes the years fly by and to be honest run together. There are however, moments that seem forever burned into your memory. They tend to come in waves and I can't explain what triggers them, some good some bad. In our program, we have parents that have been around since I started coaching because I have coached as many as three of their sons. They do a good job of bringing up things from the past as well as former players telling stories when they get together. "Hey coach, you remember the time when…..?" The players tell these stories with such passion and their faces light up like kids opening presents at Christmas. Trust me when I tell you all these stories are not game winning home runs or striking out the final batter to win a state championship. Most of the time they are stories of adversity, mistakes and life teaching moments. Very few times have I ever heard them talking about individual accomplishments. Even though these things may seem trivial, they are a blessing and continually remind me of why I got into to coaching in the first place.

I would like to share some of these memories, highs and lows, with everyone so that you may see through my eyes why I feel so blessed God has allowed me to be a part of something so special. I think it is important to start at the beginning and tell these stories chronologically because so often people only focus on success and the number of championships but in reality your program, business or even your family is built on a series of actions or decisions made when we experience failure. I think when you really dig into your memories, you will find that the great times are often a result of or at least directly correlated to what you would classify as the bad times.

Infield Fly Rule: In my first year as Head Coach, we were playing in the Edgewood Tournament Championship early in the season against Macon-East Academy from Montgomery. We had a three run lead going into the last inning and dropped three fly balls that never left the infield with runners in scoring position and lost the game. So what did we do on Monday? I turned the sound system on as loud as possible and we hit fly balls to the infielders for hours. We hit them tennis balls so they were harder to catch and did sprints between rounds. I very rarely get mad about a physical mistake which my player's will attest to. You will never see me take some one out in the middle of an inning for making an error. Mental mistakes on the other hand are very hard for me to accept because it's something you can control. "Chance favors the prepared mind!" It's all about intense, controlled focus.

Ball off the Head: Also, in my first year as a Head Coach, having already won the first game in the State Semi-Finals, we were leading Macon-East, 5-0. Kyle Tidwell, had hit a grand slam in the first inning and we were cruising. By the 7th inning however, we only had a one run lead with two outs and they had runners at 2nd and 3rd. A routine ground ball hit to our 2nd baseman, Drew Edwards, who by the way had not committed an error all season. So of course, what happens, a bad hop, the ball goes off his head into right field, both runs score and we lose the game! You see these types of things happen in baseball all the time and I think that's why I love the game so much. There are so many variables, Drew could not have done anything different. He did everything right and we still lost; such is life. Wouldn't you know it, we lost the next game and our season was over. In a matter of seconds, we went from sitting in the cat bird's seat, rested and waiting for our opponent in the finals, to picking up the pieces of our shattered dreams. "So close, yet so far away."

The Homerun: I told you about the ground ball off the head in the State Semi-Finals but what I haven't told you is how we made it to the Semi-Finals. We were down by two runs in the bottom of the 7th, with two runners on and two outs. In steps our Senior Catcher, William Gaston. He was leading the team in walks and hit by pitches by a considerable margin so of course I thought for sure he would crowd the plate and get plunked. Nope, first pitch he hits a walk-off three run homerun to right centerfield. I still have the picture of him being mobbed at the plate hanging on my office wall. As a first year Head Coach, I think you never grasp the gravity of a situation like that while it's happening or what it may mean to your program down the road because you're just caught up in the celebration. It's not until years later when you glance up at the picture on the wall, you truly have a real appreciation for just having being present for that moment in these kid's lives.

13 Errors: As I explained earlier about scheduling being a priority in the program, it's not just who you play but also where you play them. My 2nd year as head coach, we played Tattnall Square @ Columbus State University. It was one of the most embarrassing losses I have ever experienced as a coach. Not only did we make 13 errors and get beat 13-2, we did in front of a college coaching staff against a great program (Tattnall Square) from Macon, Georgia

and they were coached by one of my former teammates in college. I wanted to crawl under a rock and hide. As a young coach it's hard to watch this unfold and not be angry, because you think it is a direct reflection of your ability. You have stuck your neck out to get an awesome venue, promoted it in the community as two historic programs in neighboring states and you see it as an opportunity to promote what the program is all about. Instead your kids look unmotivated and have a complete lack of focus. Coaches always have a choice when these things happen and trust me when you coach for long enough, they will happen. So, feel sorry for yourself and come up with a long list of excuses or use it a building block and teachable moment to propel your team forward. So the next day, we took ground balls for hours. I made them take ground balls with no gloves, they did sprints between rounds and they even did push-ups between rounds so their arms were tired. The point was not to punish them but to make them understand there was no excuse for a lack of focus regardless of physical fatigue.

Breaking Curfew: Part of building a program is holding young men accountable for their actions. Putting rules and regulations in place is essential but enforcing them is even more critical. In 2005, we took a trip to Mobile, AL during Spring Break to play a nationally ranked team out of Louisiana and the top ranked in our association, Mobile Christian. We had played Central Private on Friday and got beat twice and were scheduled to play a doubleheader on Saturday. Curfew at the hotel that night was set for 11:00 p.m. Wouldn't you know; three starters were not in their room at bed check. Now these boys weren't out on the town or doing anything terrible, just not where they were supposed to be when they were supposed to be. One of the guys, Will Stillwell, was just sitting out in the hall talking to his girlfriend. So I benched all three of them and told them depending on their attitudes as teammates that day would determine how long that would last. We got beat pretty bad in the first game and we were losing the second game 4-3 going to the 7th. The boys I benched had sat there all day and cheered for their teammates without pouting so I pinch-hit them consecutively. We scored two runs, won the game 5-4 and went on to win 25 consecutive games for Glenwood's first State Championship in 12 years.

Throwing the Helmet: During my 2nd year on our playoff run in the State Semi-Finals, I had to sit our starting centerfielder, Brett Worthington, when he threw his helmet in disgust after making an out. For me it wasn't a tough decision because the precedent had been set and no matter what the circumstances are, the program comes first. It not being a hard decision in that moment doesn't make it an easy thing to deal with when the dust settles. When you look around and a four-year starter and two-hole hitter is sitting on the bench, it sets in. Not because you may lose because of it but because someone that has meant so much to the program is not out there with his teammates trying to achieve a goal they have worked so hard for. If you look the other way because it's the semi-finals, what message does that send your kids in the most important game of all; the game of life!

Dominant Pitching: I let the cat out of the bag about winning the 2005 State Championship but what I remember is how dominant we were on the mound against a very good team from Faith Academy. They didn't get a runner past 2nd base in both of our victories and guess who was Game 1 starter; Brett Worthington. The same guy I benched the week before was about to pitch the game of his life. Following him for Game 2, was Chris Minney and when we got to that point, the smart money was on us. You see, Chris was 44-4 for his career in high school and college, I liked our chances. He did not disappoint, throwing a complete game 3-hitter. What I also remember is how well we played defensively. Our shortstop, Eric Skinner, had as good a series as I've ever seen and was named MVP because of it. We didn't have power pitchers, we relied on pounding the strike zone, making plays, playing small ball and grinding it out. What I like about those types of teams, they are usually discipline, tough and remain focused when the pressure is on. I think about this team with such pride and couldn't imagine of a better group of young men to share my first State Championship with.

Clubhouse Eviction: In 2007, we were about 15 games into the season and we were 8-7. This was very frustrating considering we returned all but one starter from a team that lost in the Semi-Finals the year before. Not to mention we already had seven kids sign college scholarships and some would argue as talented a starting nine as the program has ever had. I began noticing a lot of complacency and to be honest ungratefulness so I kicked them out of our brand new clubhouse. Picture 20 guys in the parking lot with their cars circled up changing clothes in the middle every day. One of the parents even bought them milk crates with their names on them for lockers. We went 30-3 the rest of the way in route to a 2nd Championship in three years.

The Diving Play: In 2007 we were once again playing Faith Academy in the State Championship. They had a hard throwing right-hander, Justin Upchurch, on the mound. He was drafted by the Chicago White Sox that year and was topping out at 94 that day, so I knew this was going to be a tight, defensive game that probably be decided in the last inning on a squeeze bunt or something. Well that's what you get for thinking. We had scored 9 runs by the 5th inning; the harder he threw it, the harder we hit it. By the 7th inning we had 12 runs but we couldn't seem to slow them down either. They had bases loaded in the last inning with two outs and our shortstop made one of the best plays I have ever seen. It's kind of hard to explain, but the batter hit a soft line drive towards leftfield and Austin Allison comes out of nowhere it seemed with a full extension dive towards the leftfielder and made the catch. Honestly, I think it saved the game because they had so much momentum and if that falls in who knows what might have happened. I think what also made it so memorable for me is that he did the same thing in the Quarter-finals with the bases loaded on a ball hit up the middle that saved the game and allowed us to advance.

Drag Bunt with Big Murph: In the same series in 2007 after surviving a slugfest in Game 1, we were locked up in pitcher's duel. We had one of the best pitcher's in program history, Nathan Kilcrease, on the mound so I wasn't very concerned about them scoring much but they had a lefty that carving us up. About half way through the game I could tell he had our number and we would have to scratch and claw for whatever we could get. I have always been known as a small ball coach that takes pride in pitching and defense. However, the 2007 team probably had the most power of any team I have ever coached. We had several guys that could launch them into the trees and after we hit the ball so well in the first game, conventional wisdom may have been to wait for one of them to hit one off the wall but I just knew that wasn't going to happen. We had finally managed to get a couple guys on with a walk and error so we had 1st and 2nd with no outs. In stepped Tyler Murphy, standing 6'4, 250 pounds and could hit balls farther than any kid I've ever coached. He was actually a 1st Team All-American in Junior College. So of course you know what happened then, drag bunt! They never even made a throw on the play and now we had bases loaded, no outs and losing 2-0. Two hits later we had a 4-2 lead and finished off the State Championship Series.

Pop Fly: We were playing one of the top ranked 5A teams in the state of Florida at the end of our yearly Spring Break trip. Up by one run, two outs, runners on 2nd and 3rd, pop fly to our 1st baseman, Dudley Taylor, hits right in the palm of the glove and falls to the ground. We lost by one. Dudley was one of the best 1st baseman I have ever coached and one of the best leaders in program history so to say he was devastated would be a huge understatement. As a coach your heart truly breaks for the kid but in these types of situations you have to find words that will cauterize that wound so it doesn't fester. We didn't lose but one game the 2nd half of the year in route to the 2009 State Championship.

Throw to Leftfield: Let me set this stage for you. It's the deciding game 3 of the State Championship in 2009. We have already played two epic one run games decided in the last inning of both. We are ahead by one in the 7th inning, runner on 2nd base and the batter has two strikes. I call time to meet with our pitcher and catcher. The message is clear and concise, don't worry about the runner at 2nd base. He is the fastest guy in our association and we could care less if he steals 3rd base, just get the batter! What do you know, the next pitch he steals 3rd and our catcher throws it into left field so the game is tied and goes into extra innings.

Not Coming Out: I told you a story from that epic 2009 three game series in the State Championship and how it went into extra innings but what I didn't tell you was the starting pitcher, Jacob Livingston, threw 138 pitches to secure that final game. I have always taken pride in not over using pitchers and through the years have always been very careful with pitch counts to put the player's arm health first ahead of winning. Unfortunately, all programs don't adhere to this and guys get hurt or at the very least, wear down at the end of the season. After going to the 8th inning, he threw a few pitches, I could tell Jacob was exhausted so I went for my last visit to the mound and I will never forget what he told me. "Coach, I am never going to pitch again, please let me finish this for you!" 3 up, 3 down and the 17th championship in program history was in the books.

17 Pitch at Bat: In 2010, we had a very inexperienced team. We graduated a lot from the previous year's club so entering the state championship series we were definitely the underdogs. The team we were playing, Pike Liberal Arts, had only lost one game all season, they had their ace on the mound and he was really good. We were young but very talented and I felt if we could find a way to beat them in Game #1 with their best guy out there, that momentum could carry us through the series. We were down 2-0 in the 6th inning, just like 2007, and believe me those flashbacks were very vivid in my mind. This time we scratched two walks and in stepped, Spencer Riley, not what you would classify as an offensive juggernaut like Tyler Murphy. Spencer was one of the best defensive 1st baseman I've ever coached and a scrappy hitter but I knew he would have a tough time against this guy. To be honest I don't know why I didn't bunt him but he walked the first two guys and Spencer had done a good job all year hitting behind runners so I let him swing away. What followed was an epic battle of wills at historic Patterson Field in Montgomery, AL. He worked the count full and pitch after pitch after pitch; foul ball, foul ball, foul ball. On the 17th pitch of the at bat, he hit a ground ball with eyes as we call them and some, how found its way between the outstretched arms of the shortstop and 3rd baseman. We scored a run to pull within one and they pulled the starting pitcher. The reliever was greeted with three straight hits and we won the game 4-2. We

won Game #2, 6-5, fittingly ending on a pop-up to our catcher, Keaton Aldridge, to secure Back-to-Back State Titles and I am fully convinced the momentum from that moment carried over. That young team realized they could beat anybody on any given day.

Our Rival: Those words tend to carry a lot of weight when it comes to athletic competition. Now if you ask most coaches, this is more for the fans, newspapers and television than the people on the field actually competing but never the less it has its place in every community around the country. Each sport can have a different rival depending on what programs are competing at a high level for a few years, really close games for several years in a row with a certain school or even some trash talking within the community can earn that classification. However, most schools have a natural rivalry and it's usually determined by geographic location to your school and that you are competing for the same state athletic titles. That rival for us is Lee-Scott Academy in Auburn, Alabama. Now since I've been the Head Coach, my record versus them is 36-9, so we have definitely had the upper hand on the field but every time we play the stands are full and it's a big deal for our communities. Now, I have always had great relationships with their coaches and respect their players immensely but in 2011 we hosted our rival for the State Semi-Finals and it was nuts! We had to bring all the bleachers from the softball field for extra seating and it was still standing room only. The atmosphere was definitely different from a regular season series as it should have been with a berth to the State Championship on the line. Well our boys were ready to tune of 27 runs in two lopsided victories. This was highlighted by our lead-off hitter, Will Allison, going 8-9 in the doubleheader including hitting for the cycle (HR, 3B, 2B, 1B) in game 2. It was an amazing night!

Packed Stadium: After that amazing night in front of our home crowd in the Semi-Finals, we found ourselves in a familiar position against Pike Liberal Arts in the State Finals for the 2nd consecutive year. However, there was one major difference, the games were at night! For some reason, unbeknownst to me, our state championship has always been during the middle of the day, making it tough for fans to get to a neutral site without taking off from work. This year was different and man was it awesome. I remember looking into the stands about the 3rd inning of the 1st game and it was packed. Usually as a general rule when coaching you don't really notice the crowd because you are so wrapped up in trying to win on the field but this atmosphere definitely caught my attention. Our student section was rocking and you could feel the electricity. We lost the first game of the doubleheader but that didn't take one ounce of enthusiasm from our fans. The 2nd game was an 11-1 victory but to be honest I don't remember many details about the game, only the amazing crowd!

59 Pitch Complete Game: After the dust settled from an emotional night and the packed stadium, all focus was on a deciding game #3 for the 2011 State Championship. Throughout my career I have always tried to develop a pitcher during the season that teams we might meet in the state championship know little or nothing about. Often times it's a young guy but sometimes it's just a guy I

never throw in region games or even in our state for that matter. I do make sure whoever this pitcher is, he has pitched against good competition the entire year so he is not overwhelmed by the situation. That year it was Tyler Condrey and Pike didn't know what hit them. He was a finesse pitcher that pounded the strike zone and could pitch backwards. Our catcher, Keaton Aldridge, called a masterpiece behind the dish. We threw breaking balls in fast ball counts and vice versa. Pop up after pop up after pop up and his only strike out came on the last pitch of the game, his 59th! He dropped down and threw a side armed curveball that he had not thrown in a game all year, only during our bull-pen sessions. What a moment to have the courage to do that on the biggest stage of his life.

Shot Heard Around the World: In 2014, we faced a familiar foe, Monroe Academy, in the State Semi-Finals at home. It was a deciding game 3 after an epic 13-inning, 1-0 loss the night before. Our place was packed, all the stands were full and it was standing room only down the sidelines. We are losing 6-2 in the bottom of the 7th inning. We managed to get the bases loaded but there were 2 outs and in stepped Chad Silvani. His older brother, Chase, was part of two state championship teams in 2010 & 2011 and was playing D1 baseball at the time. I only tell you that to help people understand the pressure some brothers may feel in our program when they have not won a championship and their brother has. That being said, Chad was a great player for us and had gotten big hits over the years in clutch situations so why not now? He knew walking to the plate he would have to hit an off speed pitch, he stands about 6'5 and 240 pounds so he is a pretty imposing young man. Bases loaded with the season on the line, that's what I would throw him; curveball for strike one, curveball for strike two, chad steps out and takes a deep breath, curveball crushed over the lights in right centerfield to tie the game. The place when nuts and come to find out later one of the middle school kids watching the game from the bull-pen recorded it. It instantly went viral and the legend of Chad Silvani in Glenwood Baseball lure was born. Wouldn't you know he came up with the bases loaded the very next inning and got walked on four straight. No way, they were going to pitch to him again!

The Speech: In 2015, we were coming off a State Championship season but only had two seniors on the roster. One was Coleman Duke, that ended up playing at Berry College and has been to five different countries with me doing missions as well as spending an entire Summer in the Dominican as an intern. The other senior was Lawson Humphries. He went on to play at Georgia Southern University and currently is a Graduate Assistant Coach there. Just because you only have two seniors, under no circumstance does that mean you can't have great leadership. I have coached teams with a dozen seniors that didn't have great leadership qualities. It's not about quantity, it's about quality! These two dudes had it in spades but there is a particular memory from that season, I will never forget.

We had just lost a gut wrenching 3rd game in the State Semi-Finals and Lawson wanted to address the team. In the next chapter,

I talk a little bit about end of year speeches from my perspective and how important they can be. Well, this one I feel had an impact on our program for several years down the road. He poured his heart out on the field and those sophomores and juniors hung on every word he spoke. He had just hit into a double-play to end his high school career and he hit it as hard as you could hit a ball but he hit to the wrong place. He was Glenwood through and through. He was a three sport athlete, his mother coached basketball at the school and he had spent pretty much his entire life there. He is one of the best players I have ever coached but yet I'm not writing about that.

Despite all his accomplishments athletically, which included the State Finals MVP the year before, he wanted to leave a legacy that was bigger than that. So instead of feeling sorry for himself because he didn't have the story book ending to his Senior year, he quickly gathered his thoughts and laid it down. It was powerful, passionate and selfless! We ended up having remarkable success over the next couple of years and you can't convince me otherwise that his speech wasn't a big part of it.

My Heart Leads the Way: In 2016, we were very good and I mean very good. We finished 46-5 and ranked #19 in the country by Collegiate Baseball Magazine. We had power, speed and a ton of arms but that's not what I remember most about this team. I remember how unselfish this team was and how much they really cared about others. To say it was a foregone conclusion that we were going to win a State Championship would be a little bit conceited but to be honest, I didn't think anyone could play with us that year in a three-game series. I was right because even the championship series wasn't very competitive. I don't remember a lot from the field that day, what I do remember was after the game; our entire team face timing Coach Howard in his hospital room.

Curtis had been volunteering for a few years and basically took over as our Director of Baseball Operations. He handled our stats, social media platforms and basically provided all the comic relief we could ever need. He graduated from Glenwood and loved our school. His father was formerly the Athletic Director and Head Football Coach at our school and the football field bears his name, so to say his roots run deep would be an understatement. Well, two days prior to the championship series, Curtis had to have emergency heart surgery. It rattled the boys pretty good but I told them that the best gift they could possible give Coach Howard was two victories and they did. They couldn't get back to that locker room fast enough to call him.

It was actually so beautiful to watch teenage boys amidst maybe the biggest accomplishment of some of their lives, to care more about how it made someone else feel and to recognize how important that moment truly was. Not because they would be forever remembered as champions but because they had the ability by being selfless to lift someone up that so desperately needed them. It was just another example of how much bigger the game is than any of us.

Never Ending Series: In 2017, we had to go to Monroe Academy for the State Semi-Finals. Besides Faith Academy and Pike, I have to say they have been our most consistent nemesis over the past twenty years. We have only played them once in the State Championship, but for a stretch of four years from 2014-2017, we played them every year to determine a spot in the finals. As I documented earlier, there have been some battles that will long not be forgotten and this series was no different. Now there were some great games in the three game series but that's not why I wanted to share this moment. Of course, we did lose Game 1, which was par for the course that season, so our backs were against the wall again and just like the previous round we responded with a 2-1 victory in the nightcap. Now here is where it gets interesting. We awoke the next morning to a torrential downpour so our Game 3 was postponed. These games were in Monroeville, AL about three hours, southwest of Phenix City, and I didn't want to drive back so we stayed. If you are not familiar with this area and I am quite sure most of you are not, there is not much to do. That's not necessarily a bad thing, unless you have twenty-five teenage boys piled into hotel rooms at the Mocking Jay Inn.

Later that afternoon, the local Junior College Baseball Coach let us use their hitting facility, to at least break up the day for us. Then of course we had to hit the Catfish House for dinner and by that time, it was raining again. What are we going to do? By that time, I was second guessing the decision to stay instead of go home but much like I have preached my entire career; adversity is when you find out who you are as a man! So we did everything we could do as coaches to keep the kids engaged and just waited and waited and waited. By the time the rain finally stopped and we had a legitimate chance to play Game 3, we had taken them for a ride by the State Prison (Stay in School!), gone to a movie at the Casino (about 30 miles away) and eaten every piece of catfish in that county!

Wouldn't you know when game time finally arrived, everyone was freezing in South Alabama in May. Who would have thunk it? I actually think it was the perfect way to tie a bow on this story. It's was just another obstacle in pursuit of a dream that started at the beginning of the season for these young men. Well, this story ended with a 5-2 victory, a trip to the State Championship and a three-day journey that will long not be forgotten.

Little Man, Big Heart: In 2017, we were loaded. We had future college players pretty much at every position and most of them were seniors but there is no way to accurately paint a picture of this team without talking about the smallest one on the field. Daniel Holley, was about 5'6, 160 pounds but there was never a question who had the biggest heart on the field. Maybe he had the biggest something else but whatever you want to call it, you can't teach it. We have had a lot of great players over the years and so many of them have been clutch when it counted the most but none more than this young man. In the Semi-Finals and State Championship that year he was faced with the exact same situation on the mound both times. I don't know what the chances are of that happening but it has to be like a zillion to one! Game #2, after losing game one, so it was an elimination game. Runners on 2nd and 3rd with only 1 out and up by 1 run in the bottom of the 7th inning. Is that a big enough situation for you?

Now as a coach you always run scenarios through your mind in a game and when you have coached as long as I have, you have been in a lot of them but unfortunately I never get to pick who is in those situations on the field. If I did, it would be Daniel Holley every day of the week and twice on Sundays. It wouldn't have been any different if he was at the plate with the game on the line or if we were playing tidily winks. This kid wanted to whoop your butt no matter what he was doing because he was such an intense competitor. I already told you how big he was and he was second on our team in homeruns. Needless to say, he showed who he was and his legend was born. He struck out both guys, both times and propelled us to a Game #3, which in both instances, we won convincingly!

CHAPTER 15
OFF THE FIELD

During my time as a coach, there are not only memories from specific games that are stand out individual performances but often they are thoughts that span over several years and are strictly about the team and program as a whole. Most of these things didn't even happen on a field at all. These memories are small parts of a long journey where the destination was unwritten and the anticipation of greatness was always uncertain. That's why I've chosen to share them because when I reflect on them, they make me extremely proud to call myself a coach and why I encourage as many people as possible to serve something bigger than themselves.

Gator Valley: Very rarely do I use conditioning as punishment however, over the years there have been a few epic journeys to Gator Valley. This valley sits about a ¼ mile behind our baseball field and has become a source of pride for some and agony for others. From time to time, teams need a wake-up call when they get comfortable and it's the perfect place for it. Not only is it a 45-degree incline, it's over 50 yards long and the years have not been kind to the ole girl. Weather and erosion have given it many different face lifts and sometimes choosing your route is the most important decision of the day for a baseball player. One of the most commonly asked questions from former players is, "Coach, when is the last time you took them to Gator Valley?"

Mighty Faith Academy: Early in my career there was definitely one coach that stood out to me, Lloyd Skoda from Faith Academy in Mobile, AL. His teams were always very talented but what I loved about his teams were how discipline and fundamentally sound they were. We had some great games over the years, which included battles with former MLB American League MVP, Josh Donaldson. Most of the time they were tight games that were well pitched and featured outstanding defensive plays. He was so humble despite being a legend and gracious in victory as well as defeat. He always made time for me not only when we played each other but at state and national conventions. Despite winning multiple state championships and coaching several major league players, I always saw him taking notes at clinics, talking to other coaches about the game and willing to share any of his knowledge with young coaches. I have told him this before but I can never thank him enough for setting that kind of example for me follow. No matter how successful you are, you are never bigger than the game. As a coach, I was privileged to win my first two state championships against one of the greatest high school coaches ever but more importantly to me against a great man and mentor.

College Games: I love taking our team to college games. More times than not it is to watch one of our former players and we usually do this around our scheduled road trips when it's feasible. They not only get to maybe see a former "Glenwood Gator" they look up to, but gain a greater appreciation for what it takes to get to the next level and how the speed of the game changes. It is also another way to let college coaches know you run a first class program and are serious about getting your guys to college. It's also never a bad thing to hang out with my dudes!

Team Camp: I believe anytime as a coach you have the opportunity to get your players away from home and out of their comfort zone is definitely a good thing. Team camp is perfect for that. They have to be up at a certain time, get to breakfast, lunch and dinner on time and adhere to dorm curfew. It's all about accountability. Mommy is not there to wake them up, wash their clothes and buy them snacks. In addition, it's usually 95 degrees in the summer where we live so they are tested mentally and physically by a full schedule of practicing and games. Depending on where you chose to take your guys, there should be ample opportunities for team building exercises. We have been to many different colleges and universities but for the last several years we have gone to Berry College in the North Georgia Mountains. It's where a large part of the movie *Remember the Titans* was filmed (such a beautiful place). As a team, we hike to the top of the mountain where all the upcoming seniors must address the team. These seniors give their expectations for next season and tell everyone what the Glenwood Baseball Program means to them. It is a chance for the younger guys to really see how important this whole process is and what they are a part of.

Community Service: I have such great memories over the years from events we have done in our community and even communities around the world. We have volunteered at homeless shelters, done grounds maintenance for battered women's shelters, helped with disaster relief efforts, worked with the child advocacy center and even helped build a home on "Extreme Make-over Home Edition". However, one of my favorite experiences had to be Quitman County HS. Quitman is about an hour south of us, just across the state line in Georgia. It is one of, if not the poorest county in the state. I met their Head Coach the year before when we invited them up to play at our place. I knew their situation and just wanted our kids to realize that unfortunate circumstances are everywhere and could be right under your nose but people just turn a blind eye because let's be honest; it's easier for people to just look the other way. With the help of the booster club, we fed them and donated equipment to them after the game but while this was happening, I just fell in love with their coach, Felix Galloway.

Definitely one of the nicest men I have ever met. He is a volunteer, in his seventies and all he cares about is showing those kids love while trying to instill discipline that will help change their perspective. We spent two days down there during the summer, completely renovating the playing surface, administering clinics and donating equipment. There was a lot of help from the local community and when we were finished working, everyone hung out and ate together at the community center. Coach Galloway stills calls to check on me and he never finishes the call without praying for me first.

Each and every time I have been so proud to be a part of any effort to make our community or other communities better but selfishly being with my guys while doing it, brings a level of joy I can't truly explain in words. When you actually witness with your own two eyes a noticeable change in a young man's perspective on life, it humbles you beyond belief. Seeing young men and women in other countries being put in uncomfortable situations and figuring out how to become comfortable gives me hope for a new generation of servants that understand the importance of putting others ahead of themselves.

End of Year Speeches: If you ask any coach, one of the hardest things in the world is knowing what to say on the field to the guys/girls when that last game is played and their season is over. When that finality hits the seniors square in the mouth and something they have poured so much of their life into is gone, it can be a very emotional time. Fortunately for us, we've won our last game several times so it does make it a little easier to bear when everyone has tears of joy from finishing on top. Even then, I think it is extremely important to choose your words wisely when addressing your team because you will never get that moment back to make a life lasting impression. For the most part, I feel your words need to be positive in nature but above all else, honest. Through the years I have always thanked our kids for their service to our program, their dedication and what they mean to me as a person. However, there was one season when I called out the seniors for their lack of leadership and selfishness because I felt it was with-out a doubt necessary for them going forward as young men. I am happy to say that to this day, I am as close to some of those players as any I have ever coached. There is one quote I specifically remember telling a team after we lost a tough three game series in the State Semi-Finals, "Baseball does not define who you are, it teaches you the man you can become"!

Banquets: End of the year ceremonies are done differently everywhere you go. Some have dinner, some give out individual awards and certificates but what all of them have in common is recognizing student-athletes for their achievements on the field. I have always felt it's important for the parents to maybe see a side of you they wouldn't normally see. For the most part, they observe you at games in the heat of athletic competition and not on a daily basis at practice, community service projects and team functions when your true relationship is developed with their son or daughter. Now I am not really a proponent of individual awards, I am more in favor of senior and team type awards but I do always talk about the players and their contributions to the program. It is also imperative that you recognize the sacrifice parents make year after year for your program to be successful and certainly never forget to thank your wife! When talking about your players, it's ok to get emotional because that's real. Trying to hide that doesn't paint a true picture of who you are and man over the years we have had some tear jerkers. One of the greatest compliments I have ever received as a coach came at one of my former players' weddings. During his dad's speech, he thanked me for teaching him it was ok to cry in front of people.

Facility Upgrades: I think it is extremely important to stress improvement, not matter how great or small. I also feel sweat equity is a key ingredient to developing long lasting pride in any program. For our program, I had a five-year plan to begin with and stuck to it. Whatever it took, whomever I had to beg, however many fundraisers it took and however many hours of back breaking work was required, we were going to do it together. We carried cinder blocks, shingles, trusses, siding, plywood, beams, and laid sod by hand. There have been thousands of hours over the years from coaches, players and parents dedicated to our vision. No matter how great our facility looks, we want to ingrain the mindset of never being satisfied. It may only be one small project a year but its progress none the less. If we are not going forward, we are going backwards. Because of this mindset, we have one of the finest high school facilities in the country (2011, ABCA/Turface High School Field of the Year).

Conventions: It's well documented how crucial I think attending conventions are to your continued development professionally. If you don't believe me, just ask my assistants. I have seen, who I consider the best coaches in the country, consistently attend and immerse themselves at these events year after year. Obviously attending State Conventions are more feasible for most due to proximity and budget but attending the National Convention is an entirely different level. When I first start coaching, Phil Stillwell was part-owner at The Game Headwear Company and they always attended as a vendor. He asked me if I wanted to go with him because he thought it would be a great way for me to meet college coaches and help promote our program. I couldn't say "yes" fast enough. He introduced me to so many coaches and gave me such an amazing opportunity to not only grow our program but develop myself as a young man searching for inspiration. He has been become one of my dearest friends to this day and he will never truly understand how much that meant to me.

I would be remised if I didn't share a few stories from these adventures with you that have had a huge impact on my life. When

I first started attending, Phil, introduced me to Gene Stephenson, the 3rd winningest coach in NCAA Division I history. This guy is on the Mount Rushmore of college baseball coaches. We went to dinner every year during the convention and to be honest, I was like a little school girl, with her first crush on the star quarterback. Man, I hung on every word he spoke. Like most successful people, just as humble as he could be and his stories were legendary. He probably got tired of me asking questions but you would have never known it. If you are not familiar with his story, I suggest you do some research because he is a baseball program architect in every sense of the word.

He was an assistant at the University of Oklahoma in football and baseball during the late 70's before he took the Head Baseball job at little known Wichita State University. He signed a month-to-month contract and they didn't even have baseballs. How much confidence did he have in himself to take that leap of faith? He went from having all the bells and whistles to not having a bell or a whistle. Well, all he did was build one of the premiere facilities in the country and mind you, this was before Universities were building all these big stadiums. He was a regular at the College World Series and also paved the way for pay increases in college baseball that were decades overdue. How do you like them apples?

Not only did I get to spend time with him at conventions, he was gracious enough to invite me over to his house when I took one of my players to visit Wichita State. We sat in his movie room and just talked baseball. What an unbelievable experience and I promise you, he has no idea what an impact that made on me. But, that's what great leaders do. They inspire without trying because it comes so natural to them. My thoughts constantly centered around his example. If he did it, why couldn't I? Why couldn't I take a small private school to national prominence? Why couldn't I build one of the nicest facilities in the country?

Another person Phil introduced me to was Tony Gwynn, maybe you've heard of him. If you haven't, we need to have a serious talk. Besides being one of the greatest hitters of all-time (HOF 2007), he also became the Head Coach at his alma mater, San Diego State University, after he retired from the Major Leagues. The convention was in San Diego one year and Phil asked if I wanted to meet him, duh! That was the first thing we did when our plane landed. I couldn't get into that rental car fast enough. I was so fidgety on the ride over because my mind was racing with what questions I may ask him. After meeting Tony and we sat down to talk, all that anxiety when away like ships that pass in the night. He was so dialed into our conversation. There we no text messages, phone calls or interruptions of any sort. It was me and him and nothing else. I was sitting in a room by myself, talking hitting with Tony Gwynn for at least an hour and a half. Do you know how much money some people would pay for that privilege?

That's how he was, first class all the way. He came to the convention a few days later to see us and he looked like the pied piper. He had a line of people following him everywhere. When he finally made it over to the booth where we were, people still just kept coming up and asking for his autograph. He was so polite and in a very mild voice, just told them, "I am visiting with my friends right now. Can you give us some time and then I will sign autographs"? I will never forget that as long as I live. But, that's how Tony was. When you were with him, you always had his undivided attention and in this day and age, that is so rare.

About a month later, I get a mysterious letter in the mail and didn't recognize the address. I had no idea what it was or who it was from. I open it to find an article on hitting and attached to it was a yellow post it note that read, "What do you think about this"? Signed, "T". Tony Gwynn had sent me an article on hitting in the mail from some random town in California and wanted to know my opinion. How cool is that? I was so sad that he passed unexpectedly in 2014. I only hope that people truly appreciated just how amazing a person he was regardless of how good a baseball player he was.

Former Players: I have been blessed to coach so many great players over the years and I will tell you that no one player has been any more important than the others. Of course from the outside looking in, it would be easy to assume coaches have a closer relationship with guys that were All-Americans, got drafted or went on to have great college careers but that is just not the case. I have always maintained that the guy just fighting to get a shot to play college baseball is just as important as the D1, no doubt prospect and equally as important is the guy that has been in our program fighting tooth and nail just to make the team and be a contributor. They are all important for so many reasons but first and foremost because they serve something greater than themselves. My former players come to visit me all the time and never once do I think about where they hit in the line-up, how many games they won on the mound, if they were All-State or if they sat the bench, only that I love each and every one of them. No matter how beautiful we make our facilities or how many state championships we win, that will never change.

As I get older, I certainly gain a greater appreciation for my former players and teams. We have been blessed over the years with so many great victories and equally as important with our share of losses. That's right, recognizing that some losses are as or if not more important than victories, is a key ingredient to becoming a successful coach and leader in any profession. "If you want twice the success, double your rate of failure", Jeff Olson. Having great mentors allowed me to develop a coaching philosophy over four years as an assistant that put many factors ahead of just winning. Winning is a bi-product of so many little things that many coaches lose sight of when allowing the "pressure" of winning to affect their decision making. I always quote Cal Ripken Sr. to my players, "If we do all the little things right, then we'll never have a big thing to worry about."

I know that I keep harping on how important relationships are but it truly is the straw that stirs the drink. You can win all the games you want, build cathedrals to play in and make all the money you want but if the relationships aren't genuine and forever life changing, then you are just wasting your time. So you get to be on TV maybe or see your name in the newspapers or in magazines and get you a big championship ring. Then, people get to tell you how good you are and then some of us may even start to believe it. I can tell you without hesitation, the late night phone calls I get from my players have nothing to do with my win/loss record or anything I have accomplished on the field, it has everything to do with "trust". They know, without question, I have their back, no matter what.

These phone calls are very rarely about baseball. When they are still playing in college, we may start off by talking about their games or practices and maybe even their coaches but that usually doesn't last long. Most of the time, when we get down to the brass tacks, it's about their relationships, family issues, being home sick or a class that's kicking their butt. Sure, I have had to talk some of them off the ledge because they are in a slump and/or they can't get anybody out but more often than not, they just need to talk about life. They need someone they trust to talk to and they know I'm going to tell them the truth. I am definitely not the sugarcoating type. It is a responsibility I take very seriously.

When they get out of college, the calls are less frequent but every bit as important. The conversations revolve around leadership and parenting for the most part. Those really get my heart pumping because it's such a critical time in their lives. We talk about their marriages, their jobs, their kids and their relationships with Christ. There is that word again, "relationship". It is the essence of everything we do that matters so why should coaching be any different. To be honest, it's the most worthwhile and full-filling part of my job. As a matter of fact, while I was writing this, I got a text from one of my former players; it was a picture of his new born baby girl. They have no idea how special those moments make me feel.

This is a text I received from one of my players, Brandon Moseley, "You managed to be the missing piece to the puzzle in a lot of aspects in my life. It's never just been about baseball. I came here and was given a chance, but you took the game of life to a completely different level for me. I'm not done and try to grow every day, but you were essential in my life for the last four years and it really does mean a lot to me. You were never scared to jump on my case when I acted dumb or was irresponsible and I respect that more than you know. I love you coach and I really do appreciate everything you have done for me."

This is a text I got from one of my parents, "Thank you for everything that you do and pour into my son. He is a better person because of you. People always ask why I took him to Glenwood and I always tell them that he would have be fine somewhere else but now he is better than fine. You have built a great legacy and program. Keep doing you! We love you!" Now that's why I coach! I would run out of paper trying to thank my former players and parents for their awesome words of encouragement over years but know this, every one of them have always motivated me to be the best Coach and mentor possible.

"Judge yourself as a coach by how many former players come to see you!"

CHAPTER 16
THE YEAR

It's really hard for me to put into words an accurate depiction of the year 2017. I think the best way to start is by saying the first words that come to mind: Mind Blowing, Inspiring, Humbling, Proud, Shocking, Grateful, Amazing, and Undeserving! It started with the release of *Serve to Lead* right before the season started. To hold something in your hand that you have dreamed about and worked so hard on for so many years is a very proud moment. I have been an avid reader since becoming a coach and I know how much those books have inspired me over the years, so thinking I could possibly have an impact on people through written words was so exciting. It also, finally allowed me to thank so many people that have pushed and inspired me to become the man I am today.

The season started shortly their after and I knew we were going to be good. We returned a wealth of talent after winning a state championship the year before and this team was as competitive as any group I've ever coached. We didn't have as much power but we were fast and had a ton of arms. We got off to a great start that year, winning 19 of our first 20 games, had a great spring break trip to Jacksonville, Florida and seemed poised to make a run at winning back-to-back titles. We were playing a doubleheader at home in April two weeks before the playoffs started when this year of my life took another crazy turn. We actually played very well in the first game against a potential playoff opponent at the time. So I was in the dugout making the line-up for game #2. Someone said, "Coach Fanning, you got a second?" Of course, before I look up, I am thinking no I don't, I am trying to make the line-up.

So I look up and I notice some people walking on the field and they aren't wearing uniforms or umpiring outfits. What is going on? The more I stand there, the more my jaw begins to drop. I see the Mayors from Phenix City and Smiths Station standing beside each other. Standing with them is the State Representative from our District and my Headmaster, Frankie Mitchum, with this grin on his face like he just stole the Hope Diamond and got away with it. As I start to walk out on the field in bewilderment, I notice this long line of former players filing in from right field. If you were watching me, my head probably looked like that of an owl, spinning completely around. Everywhere I turned, there was someone else that I noticed; my wife, my daughters, my mom, former parents I had not seen in years and there had to be about 50 of my former players there.

Tommy Allison brought out an easel that was covered up. To be honest, I was still standing there wondering what the heck was going on. By this time, my current team had lined up on the home side and my former players had lined up on the visitor's side. Mr. Mitchum started with the reading of a resolution from the Broad of Trustees, then one from the State House of Representatives and then proclamations from each mayor. The field would be forever known as Tim Fanning Field at Bill Bowers Park. As all these things are being read, I remember having these flashbacks of my girls riding on the lawnmower with me cutting the grass, helping me drag the field after games and them doing homework in the clubhouse (later I was told that there was probably more playing than homework being done). But nevertheless, all those memories came flooding back to me all at once because truth be told, that field was as big a part of their lives as it was mine. If they couldn't find me, they always knew where to look!

With all this going on I didn't even notice that Lisa Bowers was there. Her husband was a dear friend of mine (the voice of the Gators) and tragically passed away in 2014 and we named the park after him. So seeing her there brought on a huge flood of emotions because he helped me execute my vision for this program in such a selfless manner. Both of his sons, Brett and Carson were integral parts of three State Championship teams for me. I was truly honored to have my name next to him in such a special place. I cried like a baby. I am pretty sure to the best of my recollection, I hugged every single person on that field and there were a lot! It was definitely one of those rare days in your life when you just feel lucky to have been a part of something so special and unlike most days, you will never forget it as long as you live.

Well after that amazing day, it was back to reality and the task at hand. Getting ready to defend our title. In the days leading up to the playoffs, the boys were super focused and excited about their opportunity. It was one epic battle after another in every round of the playoffs. When you hear coaches say, "They don't give those championship trophies away, you have to earn them"! It was never more true than this particular year. We lost the first game of a three game series in every round that year. To bounce back every time and win the final two games shows what kind of resiliency and poise this team played with. Well I can tell this, that team earned every little gold speck on that state championship trophy and then some. I described some of these memories in the previous chapter from that magical season but looking back on it now, it was an amazing team in maybe the most amazing year of my life. If the month of May wasn't great enough already, between the semi-finals and finals, I got to watch my oldest daughter, Brianna, win a state championship in soccer. Not to pile on or anything but the week after winning the school's 22nd State Championship in baseball, Renee and I celebrated our 20th anniversary!

No rest for the weary, as I elaborated in previous chapters, we had an amazing trip to the Dominican Republic planned for the first week in June and in July, it was off to Costa Rica. We finished that amazing summer with a family trip to Aruba. If that wasn't enough joy for one calendar year, when we got back to school, I found out I was been inducted into the AISA Hall of Fame.

It's one thing to be honored by people in your community that interact with you on a daily or even weekly basis but when people from all over the state recognize your efforts as extraordinary, it takes things to a whole different level. When you decide to be a teacher and a coach, these types of things are the farthest thing from your mind. Years go by and then even decades go by and the only thing that matters to you is making a difference in kid's lives on a daily basis. When something like this happens, I think it's natural to want to reflect on your life.

Some of my first thoughts after realizing this wasn't a dream, were about my daughters. Remembering how my wife used to cart them around to all our games. Always dressed to impress but would always end up finding a dirt pile to roll around in. That's how we always rolled, together! There was nothing better in the world, than coming off that field and getting the biggest hug you could ever imagine; win or lose! See, we can learn a lot from children if we just pay attention. There were many a time I wanted to be so angry after a loss but unconditional love tends to put things in prospective for you. They didn't care if we won or lost, they just wanted daddy!

I would give anything to get those times back now but they are all grown up and now one of my biggest joys in life is getting to watch them play. Not because I want to revel in their success as athletes but to admire the beautiful, hard working women they have become. When it was time for the HOF banquet, I hoped that they felt just as much a part of this honor as I did. Without my wife and daughters support, none of this would have been possible. We hear that all the time when celebrities or athletes are accepting awards at the Oscars or the Espys:

I would like to thank my mom.

I would like to thank my wife.

I would like to thank my family.

I would like to thank my agent and manager.

I would like thank everyone that made this possible.

I definitely didn't have an agent or a manager to thank but that time old adage is 100% percent true. We don't achieve success alone. If you happen to be someone that has achieved success on your own, what does that feel like? I guarantee if you don't share in your success with others, no matter what heights you may climb to, it will be extremely lonely and unfulfilling. If you don't believe me, let's do an experiment. Pick out the five most successful people you know and ask them how they got there and I think you would be pleasantly surprised by the answers you get. If you asked me that question, the answers would be the same every time. I have only achieved success because of my relationship with God, my wonderful family, my awesome coaching staff and the wonderful student-athletes I work with every day.

If getting elected into the HOF wasn't honor enough, I was asked to speak for the entire Class of 2017. Here are a few excerpts from that speech:

"First of all I would like to start by thanking the AISA for this gracious honor. To even be in the same room and mentioned with these inductees is truly humbling. I would like to thank the entire Glenwood family for supporting me and giving me the opportunity to do what I love every day! Thank you all so much for being here tonight and sharing this with me. As I am sure all of the inductees will tell you, without our family's support, we would not be in this room tonight.

It's hard to believe it's been almost 20 years since God opened a door for me that allowed me to be around some of the best coaches in state history not because they were Hall of Famers on the field but because they were Hall of Famers off the field. They taught me how to treat people and showed me how to be humble in victory as well as defeat.

Being around them on a daily basis helped shape my coaching philosophy and allowed me to prioritize what was really important. A lot of coaches become so consumed with winning, they forget what our true purpose is: Serving Others! Ultimately it has never been about the winning for me, it's about helping young men become better husbands, fathers and leaders in our community.

When I was asked to speak tonight, I wanted to make sure my words represented all the inductees as best as possible and the words that kept coming up over and over were: Life of Service! Each one of these men and women sitting before you, have chosen a life that requires them to put others ahead of themselves for the betterment of their communities and they wouldn't have it any other way".

It was such an amazing night. So many of the most important people in my life got to share it with me and honestly that is what made it so special. In my eyes, all the sacrifices they made, allowed me to be standing at that podium. This was their award, every bit as much as it was mine, if not more!

Even thinking back on that amazing year in my life, it's still hard to fathom sometimes. I feel so underserving but if I have learned anything through the years; it's that we are all underserving of God's grace but that's why we must trust him with our lives.

"Put God first and he will bless you beyond your wildest dreams!"

CHAPTER 17
HUMBLED BEGINNINGS

I have shared small glimpses of my life with you throughout this book, however I feel it's important to share with you more about my life growing up. As I chronicled earlier, my mother was born in Foxboro, Massachusetts. Her father was a farmer and her mother a home-maker. She had five siblings and was raised in the Roman Catholic Church. Just a hard working Italian family from New England that like a lot of families from that era, valued hard work, family and faith above everything else. After high school, mom went to school to become a nurse. At age 27, she joined the Army during the end of the Vietnam War. After basic training, she was stationed in Fort Benning, GA.

While stationed there, she became pregnant with me and had a choice to make. Back then single mothers were not allowed to stay in the Army if they didn't have someone to sign as a legal guardian, so it was either give me up for adoption or keep me and be honorably discharged from the service. Not to mention, by choosing to have me out of wed-lock, it certainly caused a great deal of tension with her family back home and their strong religious ideas about marriage. Luckily for me, all she cared about was being blessed with her first child and the rest of it didn't matter to her. It was a struggle for mom from that point forward. There was a failed marriage five years later that blessed us with my sister, Charlene. This was followed by another failed long-time relationship five years later that blessed us with my youngest sister, Jennifer. Now if you ask her, she wouldn't have it any other way.

When mom discharged from the Army, she was a registered nurse so she thought finding a job wouldn't be that difficult. Well she was right but all the jobs she found were 3rd shift and being a single mother with no one to watch your child was not a legitimate option either. This began a long list of dead end jobs that didn't pay well and had no career path. She took whatever job she could get and most of the time two or three jobs to make ends meet. She worked in the grounds department for the local university, a t-shirt printing shop, cleaned houses and landscaped yards.

She had so many jobs that sometimes I don't even think she knew what day it was. She sent me to school on a Saturday when I was in kindergarten. I tried to convince her it was Saturday by turning the TV on so she could see that cartoons were on. All she said was, "Quit trying to get out of going to school". Luckily for me, the Principal had a garden at the school so he was there working that morning. After I sat there for a few hours with my Spider-man lunch box, he found me and called her to come pick me up. I have definitely used that story a few times over the years to poke fun at momma.

During a 10-year period in which my sisters and I came along, she tried to go back to school on the GI Bill but it was just too hard for her to raise three kids, work multiple jobs and do her school work. We moved a lot and I never really felt settled until I was about 10 years old. That's when I believe God really stepped in and began to show my mom the path for our family.

You have to understand by this time I had already been exposed to alcoholism, physical and verbal abuse and even sexual molestation. The neighborhoods or I should say, trailer parks we lived in on the south side of Columbus were full of drugs and gangs. I had witnessed a kidnapping and saw one of my friends get hit by a car. The only playground I had was a junkyard that backed-up to the trailer park. My mother was doing the best she could but the environment we were living in was a train wreck. When you see and experience these things at a young age you start to become hardened and if you aren't careful accept this as normal. Just before I turned ten, mom found a very small two-bedroom house on the east side of town. It had not been painted in probably twenty years and had holes in the walls but it was a house and not a trailer. It had a yard and not a barbed wire fence next to a junk yard. It was directly across the street from Eastern Little League and walking distance from East Columbus Boy's Club and Edgewood Elementary School.

When I talked to my mother about this time in our lives, her response was simple. "I have asked forgiveness for mistakes as a parent many times and during that time soon realized with God's help and unconditionally love for my children anything is and will always be possible while serving at the right hand of the father."

As she said those words to me, I thought about myself as a parent and the mistakes we all make when trying to raise our children. Everyone by nature wants to provide more for their children than what they had growing up but sometimes I believe that's where most our mistakes begin. When we focus on providing materialistic things, we lose sight of the fact that we are not in control. Our job as parents is to provide a loving environment, encouragement and teach our children right from wrong but most importantly that God has a path for all of us.

When I look back on my life to this point, that time period always seems so crucial to how my life has turned out and the journey I have been on ever since. Our neighborhood had lots of kids, we played football, baseball and basketball all the time. We built forts in the woods, looked for crawdads in the creek and road our bikes until the wheels fell off. It was such a change for me. I didn't feel like I had to constantly look over my shoulder for something bad that was coming. However, my mother wasn't very pleased when we dug big holes in the back yard to hide in when we were playing war (just like in the movie Red Dawn). I hope most of you know what I am talking about. She was even more upset when she realized we used her Christmas ornaments as grenades. To be honest, it was so much fun I didn't even care that I got in trouble. Now that wasn't always the case, my mom was no joke when it came to spankings. A push over, she was not!

One time she chased me with a coat hanger. Now, I don't remember if that was because she found out that I jumped the fence at the airport to watch the airplanes up close or when I got a little too big for my britches and laughed at her when she tried to spank me. Well, I never did that again because that dang coat hanger didn't feel too good but I also know where my love of airplanes came from. She used to take me to the airport when I was little to watch the planes land. We would sit there for hours so truth be told, it was her fault right? Of course, I am kidding but I love thinking about those days. I was definitely an adventurous young man and didn't have much fear. One time, I climbed a local TV station tower because someone dared me too. You know how high those things are? How in the world did she put up with me?

I mentioned earlier the impact being introduced to my first male role model had on me while playing Little League baseball. What I didn't mention was the impact, Butch Sanford, the director of the Boy's Club had on me. Not only was the Boy's Club like a second home to me, it introduced me to so many different things. I had never swum before, tried pottery, art, ping pong or bumper pool. These things seem very trivial now as an adult but growing up where I did, they were so extraordinary at the time. It really opened my eyes to a world I didn't know existed. I remember Butch really showing an interest in me and whether he knows it or not, demonstrated several leadership qualities that would certainly help me for many years to come. When raised by a single mother, there is a lot of alone time after school. We didn't have cable or air conditioning so I certainly wasn't go to stay in the house and I am sure the Boy's and Girl's Clubs are that place for thousands across

America on a daily basis. I'm quite certain I have showed you that I wasn't the best at filling my downtime as a kid constructively. I would hate to think what I might have gotten into if I didn't have that place to go to.

Growing up, I don't ever remember resenting people for having materialistic things I knew I would never have. We were on food stamps and received free lunches at school but that was just normal. It wasn't uncommon for me to come home to find another family living with us because they had nowhere else to go and my mother couldn't say no. I had grown accustomed to sleeping on the couch anyway. Most of the trailers we lived in were only one bedroom anyway. I guess that's why I still like sleeping on the couch. Old habits die hard, I guess.

In high school we moved to the north side of town to a bigger house. Only two small space heaters made it interesting in the winter and I do remember my mother falling through the floor while in the bathtub one time. We had holes in the floor so it was definitely interesting when the wharf rats came to visit from the bamboo patch from time to time. That's why I always get a kick out of someone when I hear them say, "I just saw a rat". I just laugh and tell them that it was definitely a mouse, not a rat! If you have never seen two wharf rats trapped on the same huge trap before, you are just missing out on life. That image has and always will be forever burned into the memory banks.

When I moved away to college, my mother was selected for a new house from Habitat for Humanity. The location was back on the south side not far from where my life began so it was a high crime area but never the less, it was really cool to see her receive such a blessing and the feeling of pride she carried to finally have something of her own. I don't know if people realize this but if you are selected to receive one of these houses, you have to contribute 500 hours of labor, at least you did back then. It was awesome to see how many people from the community came out to work off her time owed. I guess that says a lot about my mother and the impact she had on people. When I run into to people from my childhood, the first person they ask about is my mom. She has been in that house almost 30 years now.

I do think these experiences motivated me to stay focused on what I wanted in life. I will tell you that one of my favorite shows on television was "Lifestyles of The Rich and Famous". I can still remember the host, Robin Leach's, voice to this day. Just because I didn't resent not having fancy cars and mansions in exotic locations, doesn't mean I wasn't a dreamer. Now of course as I have gotten older and God's Path has been laid out for me, I understand these things are not what will ultimately make me happy. I understand that happiness is relative to the manner of life you lead and your perspective on every day that you are blessed with breath in your lungs. I have seen kids living in extreme poverty with just as big a smile on their face as a Hollywood actor on the Red Carpet at the Oscars!

In my life for example, I never felt bitter that we didn't have air conditioning, central heat or cable television. I think it gave me a greater appreciation for those things later in life. When I got to college and you added three meals a day on top of that, I didn't think it could possibly get any better than that! I might as well have been living in Beverly Hills or the Hamptons. When I needed a snack at night, I could always scrounge up a peanut butter and bologna sandwich (gross right). That's what all my teammates said anyway but think about it; big ole jar of white label peanut butter and a huge pack of one-dollar bologna, you are set! I didn't know any different and I bet you one thing, I didn't go hungry.

Sure there was no spending money or a mode of transportation but you just adapt and make it work. I never had those things before so I guess you don't miss what you never had in the first place. My mom always brags on me for never asking her for money, clothes or anything for that matter. I knew it wasn't available so I didn't ask. Besides, I had seen her work so hard to provide what she could for us, why burden her with anything else, she had enough on her plate. If I wanted something bad enough, I would pick up a job and get what I needed.

The only time I came home was when I could convince one of my teammates to come stay with me for a few days. I will admit, seeing the look on my friend's faces when there was a drug march in the neighborhood or two crack heads in my front yard was priceless. Knowing what I know now, that was an invaluable experience for those guys to see a part of society they had only heard about or seen on television but never experienced for themselves. I always knew growing up how to evaluate true friendships without fail. If they came to my house and still wanted to hang out again, they were a keeper. You never know how someone is going to react to roaches, wharf rats and a less than stellar selection of creature comforts. That goes for girls as well. My wife passed that test with flying colors. Now I will say it didn't hurt my feelings any when they invited me to come stay the weekend with them either. Sliding away from reality for a brief moment is not always a bad thing as long as it doesn't last too long!

After reading Malcolm Galdwell's, Outliers, I began to really question why and how I've become who I am today. He explains understanding successful people and how we have come to focus too much on their intelligence, ambition and personality traits when we should focus on the world that surrounds them including their culture, their family, their generation and their experiences of their upbringing. As I was reading, I found myself searching for answers why I have been so blessed with success professionally and personally despite my circumstances growing up. Some way or another we always had food on the table, a roof over our heads and clothes on our backs despite the fact the family finances on paper showed that as being, impossible. If we would have never moved down the street from the Boy's Club and across from Eastern Little League, would I have ever play sports? Would I have gone on to play college and professional baseball and received a free college education? Did growing up in these communities give me an overwhelming desire to travel around the world serving others? However, the more I thought about it, the one outlier that was missing for me was "God's Path".

I believe everyone in this world has an opportunity to be successful regardless of their outliers but so often our ideas of success are tainted by the world's definition of it, not our own. Only your effort and your heart can change your circumstances. Never look to others for true fulfillment but look inward so that your joy can be shared with everyone you may come in contact with.

"Hope to Ignite Inspiration that will last for Generations to come!"

CHAPTER 18
DIRT ROAD

Every great leader needs their own dirt road. This is the road less traveled where so many life changing decisions are made. Unlike the nice paved roads that are clearly marked and have turning lanes, this road often has no signs. It doesn't have a traffic light with a green arrow pointing you in the right direction. Instead, it has uncertainty, self-doubt and second guessing. Not to mention the pot-holes, rocks and dust that make it very difficult to navigate. What it does have is a purpose! The easy thing to do is "follow the crowd at chow time" and be the "status quo"! God has given all of us the ability to be so much more than that. Everyone has the ability to lead by serving others, but it's only by getting rid of the world's perception of you. Leaders do not care about what other people think of them because they serve something bigger than themselves. Matthew 7:14 - "How narrow is the gate and difficult the road that leads to life, and few find it". (Holman Christian Standard Bible)

There are so many parallels when it comes to athletics and our walk with Christ. As a coach we work so hard to get to the top and any successful coach will tell you the same thing; getting to the top is the easy part, staying at the top is what separates a "Great Team" and a "Great Program"! I think the same is true in our faith. The easy part is to except Christ as your savior after a great sermon and alter call or even in a small group where you feel comfortable confessing your sins and asking forgiveness. The hard part when the dust settles is your daily walk. When you look yourself in the mirror and have to ask, "What have I done to further his kingdom today?" If you have played sports at a competitive level, I am quite sure you have had a coach or two tell you to go home and look yourself in the mirror and ask a very simple question, "Am I doing everything I can?"

The same is true with God, are you working hard at it every day or just when it's convenient? Are we only praying during times of crisis or truly delving into the word? Are we sharing with others and most importantly with our own families? If you are an athlete and only train when you are told to or when you think it's expected, you will never achieve ultimate success on or off the field. So why should it be any different in our spirituality; well it's not! The leaders we all aspire to be no matter the profession all have one thing in common, their path. They find it, commit to it and stay on it! No matter the obstacles, outside expectations, setbacks, negativity or how winding it maybe, that "Dirt Road" is theirs and theirs alone. James 1:12 – "Blessed is a man who endures trials, because when he passes the test he will receive the crown of life that He has promised to those that love him." (Holman Christian Standard Bible)

Life has always been more than a game to me. Now what do those words really mean? I think the beauty of those four words is that they encapsulate so many different things. Those four words can mean something different for everyone and mean the same thing for no one. From an athlete's perspective, I am sure it often finds reference for them on the field or court during a game or practice. In reality it encompasses so much that has nothing to do with athletics but everything to do with how we see, view and even evaluate our lives. Does our life truly have meaning? If so, it has to be more than a game.

I see so many people on a daily basis consumed with their favorite college and/or pro teams. They literally worship players as if they saw one of them "part the Red Sea". Their entire weekend revolves around that team's game schedule and sadly enough their success or failure. I have never understood how someone's happiness or attitude could be determined by something they have absolutely no control over. Make no mistake, I love college football as much as anyone and love having people over in the fall for cookouts and great fellowship but I can promise you this, if the team I pull for doesn't win the game, I won't lose a moments sleep over it. For years, I have made light of these types of situations when someone I am talking to makes reference to a game that "they" lost or "we" just couldn't get anything going. My response without fail is, "What position do you play"? Immediately the conversation turns in a different direction. I know that sounds harsh but I promise my only objective is getting people to think differently. There are enough people in this world that think the same way and say the same things; be different!

I only bring up that example because people's identities seem to be tied to other people's achievements or lack thereof. I don't understand that way of thinking. That is their road not yours. The same can be said about how we dress, where we like to eat, how we choose to decorate our homes and even what type of music we like. Why would you care what people think about your choices if these things make you happy? The answer is, you shouldn't! If it's: traveling, playing golf, hunting, painting, exercising, cooking, or volunteering. If it makes you happy then do it. Our lives are hard enough to navigate without adding more "noise" to them.

I have always told my kids that life is actually pretty darn simple. Make your bed, flush the toilet and hold the door open for people. I know that may be over simplifying things a bit but I think you get the point. Quit over complicating things! We have to choose our own dirt road and not live through someone else. Never listen to the negativity. People will always try to knock you down out of petty spite or jealousy and they don't even know you, so why listen to them.

See, here is the thing and this is so important for people to understand; regardless of how much God's blesses us with, the Devil will always try to drive a wedge between us. His sole purpose is to make us second guess that relationship, so that it would cause poor decision making on our part; greed, lust, drugs, crime, infidelity, anger, alcohol, etc. You can insert whatever you want into that sentence and I promise you, it's in the Devil's playbook. Our job as Christians is not to be perfect because none of us are and never will be but it is our job to recognize his grace, ask for his forgiveness, never forget that everything we have has been so graciously given to us and can just as easily be taken away.

God made us all perfectly imperfect! We all look different and act different but yet all of us have the exact same chance to receive God's eternal salvation. It doesn't matter where you are from, how much money you have or the color of your skin. Stay focused on what your heart is telling you and always do the right thing. There will be distractions, highs, lows, wins and losses but this "dirt road" will take you wherever you need to go if you just trust the path God has put you on.

"Caring what people think, prevents you from reaching your potential as a human being!"

ABOUT THE AUTHOR

Tim Fanning has been in education for 22 years. In 17 years as a Head Baseball Coach at Glenwood HS in Phenix City, AL; he has won 8 State Championships and as an Athletic Director amassed 32 State Championships in six different sports. During this time, he has coached numerous All-Americans, had nationally ranked teams and sent 84 of his former players on to play at the collegiate or professional level. Coach Fanning is also the Founder of "Serve to Lead", a non-profit organization that uses athletics and Christ as vehicles to impact lives domestically and around the world through field construction, equipment donations, instructional clinics, bible distribution and community service volunteering in hopes of inspiring a new generation of servant leaders.

He was raised by a single mother in Columbus, GA where she instilled in him at a young age that a life worth living starts by serving something bigger than yourself. With that strength of encouragement from home, he overcame impoverished circumstances, physical and mental abuse outside the home to finish near the top of his class in high school, then go on to play college and professional baseball and receive his Master's Degree in Sports and Fitness Management.

His most recent battle has been with Stage 4 Colon Cancer. During this journey, he has inspired a community by continuing his life-long ambition of serving something greater than himself while facing seemingly insurmountable odds. Tim Fanning currently resides in Smiths Station, Alabama and is surrounded by his loving wife Renee and his two beautiful daughters, Brianna and Macie.

TO LEARN MORE, VISIT:
SERVETOLEAD2.COM

Made in the USA
Columbia, SC
03 March 2021